**"I'M ASTON|**           at
I thought was
That's what I e............. ........ .... .. .. ...... ........,
simple presentation of a complex subject.

- J.JONES

**"A SUPERBLY CRAFTED BOOK** … What
is extraordinary about this book is its clarity
and simplicity – not an easy feat given how
complex human beings can be, especially in
our sexual desires and relationships.

- F.WATCHER

**"BLEW MY MIND** … This book makes you
question everything you've ever learned about
what relationships should be like, and
ultimately offers a better alternative. Sex 3.0
may well change your life. A must read!

- MARK

**"BREVITY, CLARITY AND VISION** …
reading the book helped me give voice to my
long-held but unspoken gut-feeling about the
nature of relationships.

- JPS

**Note :** IF YOU ARE READING SOMEBODY ELSE'S COPY OF THIS BOOK (OR YOU ARE VIEWING AN ONLINE PREVIEW WHICH ONLY SHOWS A FEW PAGES) AND WOULD LIKE TO RECEIVE THIS FIRST 15 CHAPTERS OF THIS BOOK FOR FREE, JUST VISIT THE OFFICIAL SITE AND LEAVE YOUR EMAIL ON THE HOMEPAGE

**http://sexthreepointzero.com**

# Sex 3.0

## A Sexual Revolution Manual

## By J J Roberts

# CHAPTERS

# *Dedication*

This book was inspired by the women I have been fortunate enough to have in my life. It is dedicated to them, especially my mother.

# Acknowledgements

Special thanks and acknowledgements must go to Johnny, Rosie, Sasha, Ryan, Kara and Bob for everything from inspiration, encouragement, a spare sofa to sleep on, help with editing and proof reading to a good kick up the arse when I needed it to get me to finish writing the book.

*Preface*

This book was written in a fairly unconventional way.

In August 2009 I put clothes, toiletries and my not-so-faithful laptop into my backpack, and embarked on a round-the-world trip. The plan was simply to head west from London and keep going until I got back to London again. Several motherboard failures, battery failures and a new laptop later – as well as many, many countries later - this book was born.

So this book is a child of many places. Parts of it were written at the end of the world in snowy Patagonia, parts in the eternal spring of Medellin, in sultry Mexico, overlooking Ipanema beach, and during a break from the delightful chaos of the SFSX music festival in Austin, Texas.

At times L.A. provided the backdrop and inspiration, as did Machu Picchu, Sydney harbour, Hong Kong bay, Boracay white beach and the ancient city of Petra.

An exchange I had quite a lot with people during my round-the-world research was this:

"You are writing a book about relationships? What does it cover? What kind of relationships?"

"Well, it covers everything - all relationships but mostly sexual relationships."

"Covers all relationships? Damn! That must be a huge book!"

The thing is that it isn't. The aim of this book is not to provide more and more information across thousands of pages. Information overload does not clear away the confusion.

The aim of this book is to provide more clarity.

As such it is written in accord with what I call "Pure Form Theory." Pure Form Theory states that you can take something which appears to be complex – like relationships – and filter, simplify, compress and purify it, then filter it some more, simplify further, and purify and compress it over and over again until you have its simplest and purest form, expressed with the fewest words possible. You will find an example of pure form theory in action as early as chapter 4 of this book.

*"Simple can be harder than complex: you have to work hard to get your thinking clean to make it simple. But it's worth it in the end because once you get there, you can move mountains."*

*Steve Jobs*

In total, the research during the writing of this book took place across more than 40 countries, during more than two years of travel.

This book is not written in a dry academic style, and if you are offended by the occasional swear word, perhaps this book is not for you.

Also it is not specifically written for men or women, nor is it written for any particular sexual orientation. It's written for everyone, includes everyone and covers the big picture. Rather than make the book unreadable by constantly writing things like "he / she," the sexual pronouns can just be interpreted to suit yourself and your situation. Common sense makes it clear where things don't apply to you.

This book covers quite a lot of large concepts, and you might find a lot of its conclusions somewhat counter-intuitive. As these conclusions are presented in concentrated "pure form," you may benefit from reading the book in more than one pass and you might get more from it if you take notes and read it again some weeks or months later.

A lot of what I say is also counter-doctrinal and goes against what society has taught you your entire life.

Bearing in mind the fine mess we have gotten ourselves into as a society when it comes to modern-day sexual relationships, this might not be a bad thing.

*"The future of the world will not be determined between nations, but rather, in the relations between men and women."*

*D.H. Lawrence*

# 1 – This Book Is Not a Book

This book is a map.

It may not look like a map but it is.

Maps are foldy-outy kinds of things with pictures and symbols, and this is more of a page-turny kind of thing with text that may lead you to the conclusion that it is a book, but trust me it is not.

It is a map.

Ever heard the expression "the map is not the territory?"

This well-known expression was coined in 1931, I believe by a Polish-American philosopher and scientist called Alfred Korzybski.[i]

What this phrase means is that although a lot of people think that their sense of reality is the reality itself, it is not. Their sense of reality is the map, and reality is the territory. Map and territory are two different things which may correlate closely or may not.

People confuse their map with the territory that the map describes all the time.

Whenever you hear anybody say "The truth is…" followed by a subjective comment or a statement of their opinion, that is exactly what they are doing.

Let's say you are walking around a city with a map in your hand. You see a small park on the map and you head on over to the park. When you arrive, the park is not there and it has been replaced by a set of office buildings and a car park.

You would not look at the map and insist that the map is right and that reality is wrong. You would just assume that your map is out of date.

The map is not the terrain.

People carry around all kinds of mental maps in their heads about how the world works--maps concerning all kinds of things like politics, religion, relationships and so on.

Everybody carries around a map in their head called the "this is how sexual relationships work" map, and it is precisely this map that we are concerned with here.

Everybody is born with a "this is how sexual relationships work" map and when they are first born it is blank.

Children ask questions about absolutely everything because they don't understand what is going on around them. They are trying to fill in their maps. So many things are mysteries to them. Everyone starts with a blank map about many things, and they need to fill it in to survive.

Typically, as children get old enough to observe how mummy and daddy relate and react to each other, parts of their map get filled in. Being told fairy tales and bedtime stories about the beautiful princess and the dashing prince charming fills their map in a little more. Listening to the lyrics of love songs fills in their map a little more, as does watching romantic comedies.

Gradually, even though the children are not ready to start using their map yet, they develop a clear set of expectations and ideals.

When children grow up and become young men and women they embark on their own relationships. These experiences colour their maps too.

Just like everyone else, I have a "this is how sexual relationships work" map.

I am not so arrogant as to claim that my map is better than your map, but my map is almost certainly different from yours. Since you are reading about sexual relationships, then it would be fair of me to assume that you are interested in improving your map, so let's see if I can help in that regard.

Over the course of this text I will highlight ways in which people's maps come to be very badly drawn. I am going to be highlighting mapping mistakes and detailing the reasons how and why these errors get on the map in the first place.

If you don't like having your idea of reality being screwed with, then I have good news and bad news.

The bad news is that by reading Sex 3.0 your idea of reality may be completely screwed with. But hey--all your life society has been screwing with your map and your concept of reality in a bad way; taking your map further away from the terrain. The good news is that Sex 3.0 aims to reverse that.

So I am going to screw with your sense of reality in a good way, as long as you want your map to reflect the terrain more accurately.

Hell, if I do my job correctly, by the end of the book you will be ready to completely shred your own map and you will be in possession of a brand new map that is a far better representation of the territory.

I am not going to redraw your map for you. If I did that then the responsibility for your map would be mine and you would be abdicating responsibility for your love life by foisting it onto me.

You are responsible for your map--nobody else. You are responsible for your love life, not me.

So, no I am not going to redraw your map for you but I am going to help you redraw it for yourself.

# 2 – Why Relationships Seem Difficult

When children become young men and women and embark on their first relationships, they often realise that relationships are not quite like the fairy tales they were told as a child.

This can be quite a crushing disappointment, and in the absence of access to a better map, they convince themselves that the person they loved so much was at fault. They become sure that person was not the fairy tale concept of "the one" that they have been taught, and they plough onwards with a new relationship.

In other words, they insist that their map is correct and that reality is to blame.

To avoid repeating the same mistake of choosing the wrong partner, and to find "the one," they also read advice columns, talk to their mates down at the pub, read magazines, and turn to popular culture like slushy ballads and TV soap operas.

Unfortunately this compounds the problem and takes the map not closer to reality, but further away-- and here is why:

Society at large promotes a key concept which I am going to call "relationship duress."

Let's look at two definitions. Firstly, "duress," which is defined in the dictionary like this:[ii]

**du•ress** - *noun*

> *1. Compulsion by threat or force; coercion; constraint.*

> *2. Law: such constraint or coercion as will render void a contract or other legal act entered or performed under its influence.*

> *3. Forcible restraint, especially imprisonment.*

Secondly, "relationship duress", or RD for short, which I am going to define as the collective term for the myriad ways in which society creates an uncomfortable environment for those who do not seem to be following the standard script of:

> 1 - Find partner

> 2 - Date in a "committed" monogamous relationship

> 3 - Get married

Relationship duress causes all kinds of mapping errors, and as I am a sexual relationship cartographer (hey – maybe I should put that on my business card!), I find this quite horrifying.

The date -> get married script in relation to other kinds of relationships is something that I will compare and contrast later in the book, but I am not against it. I merely bring up marriage here as a way of introducing the concept of relationship duress, because it is RD that causes and perpetuates most of the mapping errors in sexual relationships, and it is the mapping errors themselves that make relationships difficult.

Relationship duress is a constant, relentless bombardment. In modern society it comes on all sides--on a daily basis--from parents, friends and complete strangers, as well as from every love song, soap opera, advice column, romantic comedy and so on.

People grow up being told that they have to "settle down" and "do the right thing." This is a form of relationship duress.

Guys are told they have to "make an honest woman" out of their girlfriend, thereby implying that a woman (and only the woman) is dishonest if she's in a sexual relationship but not married, and that her reputation for honesty can be salvaged only by the man. This is a form of relationship duress.

Even girlfriends ask their boyfriends with a completely straight face, "when are you going to make an honest woman out of me?" without realising the implications of what they're saying.

Men and women experience relationship duress in different ways, but both genders experience it for their entire lives.

Broadly speaking, there are two distinct phases of RD. The first RD phase goes from birth until marriage.

During this phase, girls as they grow up are groomed to believe in this fairy tale: that one day they will marry their prince charming, that their wedding is their fairy princess day and will be the happiest of their lives, and that they will live happily ever after.

In the meantime, guys are told that if they want a serious relationship then they have to take a women's sexuality, throw it in a box, and stamp and label the box as their property. If they don't, it's not a real relationship.

This is all relationship duress, although the "fairy princess day" part of it is the carrot rather than the stick.

The second phase of RD is from marriage onwards. When people get married, they legally handcuff themselves to each other to prevent the other from leaving should they wish to. This is clearly a form of relationship duress, albeit a mutual, one-on-one form of it. As we can see from the dictionary definition, this forcible restraint is clearly a form of duress.

Also, from the legal point made in the dictionary definition (above) of duress: *2) Law: such constraint or coercion as will render void a contract or other legal act entered or performed under its influence,* and given that it is not actually possible to grow up in society and never experience coercion to get married, you come to the amusing conclusion that, technically speaking, the contract should be null and void.

Relationship duress to have children, especially from immediate family members after the marriage, is routinely very strong also.

So the second phase of RD during your lifetime is basically:

4 - Have kids

5 - Stay married

There are countless forms of relationship duress--too many to list in this book. But now that you know what relationship duress means, you will be able to recognise it and label it as such when you see it.

New forms of relationship duress and new RD words are being invented even now, in the 21$^{st}$ century.

Recently I read a magazine article about George Clooney's refusal to settle down, where the author described him and others of his ilk who refuse to get married as "kidults"--a charmless and derisory term for a grownup who is somehow trapped in childhood and whose behaviour is deemed to be juvenile and suitable only for the immature: an adult who never "grew up."

This is a self-defeating notion, given that one of the marks of being an adult is making your own decisions about your own life and taking responsibility for them, which is exactly what Clooney did. One of the marks of being a kid is being told by other people what to do, which is exactly what the author of the article was clearly trying to do.

This is a form of relationship duress. Recognise it for what it is.

People who do submit to relationship duress go on to parrot that same RD and try to shove it down other people's throats. This is one way of convincing themselves that their own map is correct, thereby calming their own fears and doubts about whether they are doing the right thing.

The fact that they can point to so many other people in society who also are parroting the exact same RD messages convinces them even further that they are right.

"Of course I am doing the right thing," they tell themselves. "you should do the right thing too!"

Because so many people in society are reinforcing the exact same RD messages, others whose gut instincts tell them to *disagree* with the majority view become convinced that their instincts are wrong. They then forget their own better judgment, in order to conform to the majority view.

The Asch conformity experiments, which are possibly the most famous social psychology tests ever conducted, demonstrated with brilliant clarity such conformity even in small group settings.[iii]

(If you are not familiar with the Asch conformity experiments, then I strongly suggest you look up the videos on youtube.com as soon as possible--preferably immediately and before you read any further.)

If you are not online right now, I will quickly summarise: Before a volunteer sits down at a table with five other participants, he is told he is going to take part in a test of visual perception. What he does not realise is that all the other "participants" at the table are actors who are going to give the exact same incorrect answer to some of the questions, and that he is the only participant being tested for real. The real test is not about his visual perception, but about his level of conformity.

He is the only one who has a choice. He must either go against the group and give the correct answer to a visual test that was deliberately designed to be very, very easy to answer correctly--or else he must go with the group, give the same obviously incorrect answer they gave, and conform.

On more than 30% of the questions, the one real participant conformed with the group. Also, a massive 75% of participants conformed with the group on at least one question during the experiment.

When asked afterwards why they conformed, participants said either that it was because they thought the group must be right and did not even believe what was literally in front of their eyes (informational conformity); or else that they wanted to avoid the discomfort of being thought wrong or deviant by the rest of the group (normative conformity).

Conformity is this easy to achieve with a just small number of people speaking against such an obvious and easily visible truth! Just think how much easier it is to achieve mass conformity when most of the world is speaking against a truth—such as how sexual relationships should work--- that is far less obvious and less simple to understand.

The need to fit in is one of the most powerful forces in the human psyche, and is something that developed for very good reasons during the Sex 1.0 phase of human evolution. You'll read about this phase in the chapters to come.

Now you can start to understand how relationship duress and group conformity work together. Combined, these two forces take the already badly-corrupted maps that people carry around, and spread the problem. The corruption and the mapping mistakes get replicated, thereby obligating almost all others in society to accept them.

This is how the mapping errors spread like an unstoppable self-replicating virus.

This is exactly why relationships *seem* difficult. They seem difficult because everybody is trying to navigate the territory using maps that are full of mapping errors and do not reflect the territory.

What happens when you do that is you get lost and crash into things. Crashing into things is painful. In relationships the pain is mostly emotional and not physical, but arguments that descend into violence are not exactly rare either.

Sometimes you crash really, really badly and the relationship ends.

Normally when somebody has a map for a skill that can be done solo (for example, a recipe for how to make a good lasagne)--and the map is really bad--then the map gets corrected. The continued stream of failed attempts to make good lasagne will lead to the conclusion that they don't have a very good map. It will become really obvious that a better recipe makes better lasagne, so the map is corrected or replaced.

In the case of relationships, map-replacement time is when the final cruel trick gets played. It takes two to have a relationship, and presumably both are trying to navigate the territory together. But when the relationship crashes and burns and the two people are walking away from the smouldering wreckage, what they do?

They don't place blame on the maps and realise the need to change them--*they blame each other!*

They curse that "men are bastards" and "women are bitches," and lament that they must be so "unlucky" in love, and ask "Why can't I find the right person?" and tell themselves that the person they just left must not have been "the one."

Then, you know what they do? (This is the part where it gets really crazy):

*They stick the map back into their pockets!!!*

Instead of ripping up the map, burning the pieces, and stamping on what's left of the smouldering embers, they tell themselves that their map is perfectly fine! They tell themselves, "Well, I can read and navigate with my map perfectly well, so why can't I find a partner who knows how to do the same??"

Then this is what happens:

First, past failures are backwards-rationalised with favourite phrases like "you have to kiss a lot of frogs to find your prince," and …. Well, I don't know what goes here because men don't really have an equivalent backwards-rationalisation about princesses, so they have to stick with the tried-and-true "She was a bitch."

Then what?

Following a sufficient period of emotional recovery (or sometimes no recovery), people embark on a brand new journey with a brand new partner—and the exact same map! They tell themselves that it must be different this time because they are starting out on a completely new journey with a completely different person with them.

Maybe this person is "the one."

# 3 – Why Relationships Are Easy

There is one key indicator your entire life that tells you about the quality of your relationship map, and that also predicts how easy or difficult your sexual relationships are going to be.

The indicator is this:

Do you find the subject of sexual relationships, and your own experiences in them, to be troublesome, complicated or difficult? In your personal experience, would you agree that relationships are often a struggle, and that the need to "work on your relationship" is good advice?

If you do, then your map sucks.

I have got to be blunt--no pulling punches, no apologies and no, you can't be mad at me for saying so. I told you in the first chapter that I was going to screw with your reality (in a good way).

I also told you I was going to help you re-draw your map and take it closer to the terrain, and that it's totally impossible for me to do so unless I point out what I think the mistakes are on your map.

If you can help it, don't be defensive. There's no real reason to be, because lots of the mistakes on your map--perhaps even all of them—are the result of relationship duress from society at large, and were not even put on the map by you.

Also take comfort in the fact that you are not alone. In researching this book, a very common response when I told people I was writing a comprehensive book about human sexual relationships was either "Blimey that book is going to weigh a ton!" or "So, what conclusion does the book come to-- that relationships are really complicated?" Comments were often accompanied by a wince of pain and a concerned expression.

If your map presents you with an absolutely great and accurate view of the territory, then you will find it exceptionally easy to navigate with it. In other words, you will find sexual relationships to be easy, a source of delight and pleasure, and not problematic at all.

If you find that sexual relationships are difficult because you are encountering all kinds of common problems like jealousy, possessiveness, resentment, nagging issues, complacency, boredom, and a withering sexual desire for each other in the face of familiarity (followed by that desperate desire to "get the spark back"), then your map needs to be re-drawn. I am going to help you do it.

Sexual relationships are not difficult; they are easy.

Or, to be more precise, they are as easy as you make them. Make sure you have a good map, and then make the right choices based on the map, and you are good. I speak from experience.

Once you grasp this concept, it is amazingly empowering. You will begin to realise that all the stuff that society and relationship duress drew on your map is erasable. And if you don't believe you possess an eraser capable of doing that, then by the end of this book I sincerely hope that I will have handed it to you. Giving you this eraser is my mission.

To repeat: The ease or difficulty of your relationships is an option that YOU choose.

As I mentioned in the preface, this book is written in pure form style. If you skipped the preface, then basically pure form theory means: Seek clarity. Drill down. Seek clarity. Drill down more. Seek clarity and repeat over and over again. Then express the results in as few words as possible.

This mentality is essential for re-drawing the map so that it more accurately reflects the territory.

In the interests of pure form theory, and to make everything nice and simple on your map, I will tell you that "relationship" can be defined in just two words, and that there are only two kinds of human sexual relationships in existence.

Does that sound too good to be true?

Read on…

# 4 – Relationships Defined In Just Two Words

To get our map closer to the territory, we need to go back to basics and clarify the word "relationship." I will be using the word in the broadest possible terms in this chapter.

We all have all kinds of relationships in life--for example, employer/employee, student/teacher, friend/friend, boyfriend/girlfriend, landlord/tenant, customer/business owner, and so on

I had many realisations during the years of travelling, writing and researching this book, and talking to people from all different cultures. But one realisation startled and surprised me more than any other, and it is this:

People do not understand what *relationship* means.

Don't get me wrong. People have a tremendous gut-level instinct about what a relationship actually *is,* and this gut instinct means they have instant recognition of when they have a relationship in their life and when they don't; of whether a particular relationship is desirable or not; and of when a relationship is over. They just know.

It also means that they know and understand when and why some relationships are closer than others, even when relationships are spoken of abstractly about people they don't know. This is a tremendous intuitive skill that springs from a very deep level.

But they just don't think in a simple form about what relationship means. In other words, the understanding is intuitive, not conceptual.

When asked to define "relationship," most people really, really struggle and can't come up with a good definition.

Pause for a moment and try it yourself. I'll repeat here some of life's common relationships:

- employer and employee
- student and teacher
- friendships
- boyfriend and girlfriend
- landlord and tenant
- customer and business

These are all very different arrangements, and yet we apply the word *relationship* to all of them. Why?

Obviously there is some quality they have in common that makes them all a kind of relationship. So what is it?

When you ask people this question they usually come out with some vague and woolly definition like "there is some kind of emotional shared connection or bond," but that's not it. You don't need that to order a DVD from amazon.com, but you still would have a customer/business relationship with them.

So, when people already have such an amazing intuitive understanding of what the word means, then why such a struggle to define it?

Well, I have some news that might shock you.

You've been lied to your entire life. If you wonder by whom you've been lied to, the answer is: by pretty much everyone-- by society and likely even by your own family.

Lied to about what? About the nature of relationships, about what comprises a relationship, about what "committed relationship" means, and about what a "real" relationship is.

Hell, even the dictionary lies to you about the meaning of relationship!

Dictionary.com gives the following definition:[iv]

**re•la•tion•ship** – *noun*

> *1. a connection, association, or involvement.*

> *2. connection between persons by blood or marriage.*

> *3. an emotional or other connection between people: the relationship between teachers and students.*

> *4. a sexual involvement; affair*

That's not what the word relationship means. Let's look at them one by one.

> *1. a connection, association or involvement*

What if you are kidnapped one day and held in a dungeon? You would not be in a relationship with that person. Sure, you have a connection/association/involvement, but the involvement is one of kidnapper and kidnapped.

Unless you develop Stockholm syndrome and fall in love or identify with your kidnapper, then you do not have a relationship.

Therefore a connection/association/involvement with another person is not what constitutes a relationship.

> *2. Connection between persons by blood or marriage*

What if you are born a twin and, completely without your knowledge, are separated at birth and spend your entire life unaware of the fact?

Do you have a relationship with your twin? Clearly not. You are *related* – of course - but that is simply a biological fact. It could not be a relationship if you never meet or are never even aware of each other's existence.

Likewise, if there's a member of your family that you don't have contact with because you don't get along, you're related by biological fact but do not have a relationship.

Is marriage always a relationship? What if you have not had sex with your spouse for three years, live in separate houses, and are staying married "for the sake of the kids"; or staying married because you live in one of the two countries in the world where divorce is illegal; or because of the shame and scorn of your family and society at large towards divorcees? Clearly the relationship broke down a long time ago.

A marriage in those cases would be a legal entity, not a relationship. So clearly the fact of marriage alone does not constitute a relationship, even though many married people are not so unfortunate as the couples I described above, and do indeed have a relationship.

### 3. An emotional or other connection between people

Well, I'm sure you would feel emotion towards someone who kidnapped you, but it's most likely to be hatred. So simply having an emotional connection with somebody does not mean you are in a relationship with them.

### 4. A sexual involvement; affair

Most people who have been sexually abused would not say they were in a relationship with their abuser. So clearly a sexual involvement with another person, in and of itself, is not what constitutes a relationship.

So what is a relationship? Back again to our list from earlier: employer/employee, student/teacher, friendship, boyfriend/girlfriend, landlord/tenant, customer/business. Why do we use "relationship" to describe all these diverse arrangements?

What do they have in common that causes us to apply that word?

In short, what makes a relationship a relationship?

In the spirit of pure form theory, a definition is possible in just two words.

Are you ready? (drumroll.....)

*Mutual reward.*

That's it.

All that the term *relationship* means is mutual reward.

All relationships are founded on the basis of mutual reward, and all relationships break down when mutual reward breaks down.

### Employer And Employee

You get your wages. Your employer gets your time and expertise to help him grow their business. There is the mutual reward. Stop doing your job or paying your landlord, and mutual reward breaks down. You will get kicked out. If your employer stops paying you, mutual reward breaks down and you'll look for another job.

### Student And Teacher

A student gets to learn a potentially valuable skill that may help their life. The teacher gets not only the satisfaction of helping people, but if they are good, they can make a career out of it. Mutual reward.

### Friendships

Same rules apply. Strangers become friends at the (often unspoken) moment when they both realise that they like hanging out with each other.

You are friends with somebody because you both like spending time together--there is your mutual reward.

Sometimes someone likes hanging out with you but you don't like hanging out with them, or vice versa. Think you'll become friends? Clearly not.

Ever had a friend you had a falling out with, and then weren't friends with any more? The reason is that the mutual reward broke down.

You might feel the reason is the argument you had, or the falling out, or because you discovered they were dishonest. However, those and other reasons are simply catalysts for the breakdown of mutual reward.

You are not friends any more because the mutual reward no longer exists.

Ever had a friend who you think you're not friends with because you lost touch?

That is a relationship you still have today, even though you might not realise it. The mutual reward never broke down, so you still have that relationship, but just have become disconnected from it.

### Boyfriend and Girlfriend

You both get your sexual needs met and spend time together in a loving and pair-bonded bubble. Mutual reward exists.

Stop getting your needs met? Fall out of love? Argue and fight?

Mutual reward breaks down; the bubble bursts. It's not a relationship any more.

### Customer and Business

Stop for coffee at a café, sit outside and enjoy the sunshine, and then leave your money on the table and walk away--do you have a relationship with the café? Sure you do. You are a customer.

What happens if you decide to just walk away without paying? Do you have a relationship with the café then? No, even though you got what you wanted, because the reward isn't mutual.

This question of relationship is easy to answer now isn't it?

In the case of not paying, you would be a thief instead of a customer, and thief/victim is not a relationship.

So relationship is not defined as an exchange of cash for goods and services, nor is it defined as a contract (although a written contact might detail the mutual reward). Relationship is also not defined by sexual involvement, or by emotion, or by a genetic link. It is defined by mutual reward.

OK, so let's redraw your map a bit by applying pure form theory to the definition of the word relationship.

## Relationship – The Pure Form Definition

### re•la•tion•ship – noun

> 1. mutual reward

That means that relationship rules can be broken down very simply, at least when it comes to how relationships are founded and dissolved. This simplicity applies whether the relationship is personal or business, sexual or non-sexual.

### The Four Principles Of Foundation & Dissolution

> 1. If mutual reward exists, a relationship exists.

2. If mutual reward does not exist, a relationship does not exist.

3. If mutual reward is established, but mutual reward then breaks down, so does the relationship.

4. If mutual reward breaks down but is later re-established, like when you argue with your partner and later make up, then so is the relationship.

Mutual reward = relationship. They are the same thing.

## Why the confusion?

If it is that simple, then why is there is so much confusion over the meaning of the word relationship?

There are 3 main reasons

1. "Relationship" is a polyseme, which is a word with different but related meanings.

Example: If you have a sister and a cousin, clearly you are related to both of them. Are you closer to your sister? There are two different possible answers here.

If you are really good friends with your cousin and hang out all the time like best friends, and if you don't get on with your sister very well and rarely see her, you are still closer to your sister in one sense because she is a direct sibling.

However, this closeness is a level of biological *related-ness* between the two of you, rather than a *relationship* between you.

You clearly have a closer relationship with your cousin. Why? Because there is stronger mutual reward.

2. Society lies to us, or at the very least equivocates, about the meaning of the word relationship.

When somebody updates their Facebook page to say they are "in a relationship," it's a little bizarre when you realise that the word only means mutual reward. In that sense it could mean they have just bought a pet dog or found a new dentist.

Of course this does not cause confusion, because we know that society says that being "in a relationship" means to be in a monogamous sexual relationship, even though that is only one of the many, many kinds of relationships people have.

Society equivocates and tells us that this is what relationship means, because society promotes and endorses only two types of sexual relationships:

- boyfriend/girlfriend

- husband/wife

Of course these both *are* types of relationship, as long as the relationship is working out for both parties.

Why exactly society promotes and endorses these particular sexual relationships is something I cover later in the book.

3. Linguistic mist or fog, which obscures vision.

It's not unusual to hear expressions like "unhealthy relationship." Bearing in mind that the word relationship means only "mutual reward," you can see that it's not actually possible to have an unhealthy relationship. You cannot have "unhealthy mutual reward" because that is a contradiction.

You can certainly find yourself in an unhealthy *situation* when a relationship breaks down. You can even find yourself trapped in it for some time, for legal reasons or through societal or internal pressure, but that does not make it a relationship.

All relationships break down when mutual reward breaks down. If for example a marriage fails and both parties end up hating each other and contacting each other during the divorce process only via lawyers, then clearly the relationship is already over. That they are still married during the divorce is merely a legal fact.

Linguistic fog is very common in modern language.

When I address linguistic fog in this book, I will alert you to it along with an explanation--like this:

### *Fog Alert*

*Long Term Relationship*

When somebody says they are in a long term relationship (LTR), it is often understood to mean that they are in a sexually exclusive relationship.

Since relationship, however, means only "mutual reward," and long term simply means over an extended period of time, then LTR just means mutual reward over a long period of time, whether or not the relationship is sexual.

And "Long Term Sexual Relationship" simply means mutual reward over a long period of time in a sexual relationship, whether it is monogamous or not.

# 5 – A Roadmap For All Relationships

I want to clarify the fact that having mutual reward doesn't necessarily mean you have a perfect relationship. You can have relationships that are far from perfect, but nonetheless are still relationships.

Although mutual reward determines whether a relationship exists or not, it does not determine how the relationship is run or weather the quality of it is good, bad, great, awesome or whatever.

For that we need a roadmap--a universal one. We need it to cover all kinds of relationships: business, personal, sexual, non-sexual, friends and family--ALL relationships.

In short, we need what I call a pure-form relationship roadmap.

Pure-form relationships have four principles. If you like, you can think of them as four cornerstones or four pillars that hold up the structure of a building.

The stronger these pillars are, the stronger the relationship. The weaker and more damaged they are, the greater the danger of the whole thing collapsing. The four pillars of pure form relationships are:

- Communication
- Honesty
- Trust
- Respect

Let's look at a business relationship example. If you take a job and your boss turns out to be a bit of a dick who is in the habit of saying stupid, egotistical things like "remember who your master is," then you're probably not going to respect him.

Boom! There goes the fourth pillar.

In regard to the other three pillars: well, he *is* communicating but in a juvenile way, so there's damage to the first pillar. He's not being dishonest so no special problems with the second, but his other drawbacks might make you trust him less in general, so the third pillar – trust -- is damaged too.

With the fourth pillar gone, you probably won't be motivated to work very hard for that boss.

You still have a relationship because a relationship means mutual reward, and if you continue to go to work and receive your wages then mutual reward continues.

However, although you still have a relationship, you do not have a pure-form relationship. Pure-form relationships have four strong pillars, not three weak ones.

## The Universal Map of All Relationships

Applying pure-form theory for all relationships gives us a unifying and universal map that covers every possible relationship you can ever have in your entire life. We can do this in just six words.

These six words are broken down into relationship definition (two words), and relationship roadmap (four words).

*Definition – mutual reward*

*Roadmap – communication, honesty, trust, respect*

There are very few things in life that impact happiness as profoundly as the nature and quality of relationships.

Any time you feel a relationship of any type in your life is weak or in trouble, take a look at the four pillars defined in the roadmap. Where is the relationship weak? Where is it damaged? Where can it be improved?

Measuring the integrity of any relationship is a simple task that requires honestly assessing the four pillars.

How strongly do they stand? Are there cracks in any of them? Which ones do you find yourself working constantly to repair?

# 6 – There Are Only Two Kinds of Sexual Relationships

People seem to think of sexual relationships as so, so complicated. Wouldn't sexual relationships become really simple if there were only two types of them?

Great news! There *are* only two types of sexual relationships, and this chapter explains them.

Yes, only two.

You might be thinking I mean *boyfriend/girlfriend* and *husband/wife*.

Erm....no. That's what society wants you to think, and the perpetuation of that thinking is exactly what relationship duress is for.

You might be thinking that I must be leaving a lot out if I say there are only two. OK, long term heterosexual relationships are the mainstream, but what about short term relationships like casual flings? What about gay and lesbian relationships, transgender relationships, and relationships between married men and their mistresses? What about one night stands or BDSM?

Surely there are hundreds of different kinds of sexual relationships....

No, there are only two.

And these two encompass all possible kinds of relationships, leaving out nothing and nobody, regardless of gender or sexual orientation.

These two relationships are:

- Fenced

- Unfenced

Simply put, *fenced* means a sexual relationship based on the concept of sexual ownership, and *unfenced* means not based on the concept of sexual ownership.

So, examples of fenced relationships include things like conventional boyfriend and girlfriend or husband and wife relationships.

If you are thinking that by "unfenced" I must mean open relationships. Well, I don't really like the term open relationship and here is why. The opposite of open is closed. So therefore an example of a closed relationship would be a marriage.

Shops and restaurants "close." Lights out, metal shutters come down. Nobody is there.

People are not shops. We need a better term to actually reflect the dynamics of what is going on.

People don't "close" or "open," they either agree to be fenced or they don't.

When a sexual relationship is fenced, like a marriage usually is, people still find attractive people attractive. They might even enjoy attention and flirting, even if they don't act on it, and that is totally fine.

In such a scenario, such a person is leaning on the fence and enjoying the attention or flirting with someone on the other side of the fence, but is choosing not to hop over the fence while their partner isn't looking.

You could be forgiven for thinking that monogamy (one partner) equates to "fenced," and that polyamory (many partners) equates to "unfenced."

Not quite. There is a subtle but *really, really important* difference. Understanding this difference is the key.

The difference is this: it is possible to have a fenced relationship that is not monogamous, and it is possible to have an unfenced relationship with only one person.

An example of a fenced relationship that is not monogamous is swinging. Swingers are often married couples. Marriage is by definition a fenced relationship. Swingers, however, have a gate in their fence, and by mutual agreement they might open the gate to let another person or another couple in, often another married couple. Principally this is to "spice up" married sex life and help prevent sexual boredom.

It is also possible to have an unfenced relationship with just one person. This is possible because unfenced does not mean you are having sex with more than one person. It just means that there is no fence. In other words, it means there is no enforced monogamy.

Unfenced means that you are sexually free, that you don't make an agreement with anyone for sexual exclusivity. It means that if you wanted to have a sexual experience with someone else then you could, and you would not need your partner's permission, nor they yours.

It does not necessarily mean that you are polyamorous and have more than one sexual partner. It simply means that you have the option. Whether you choose to exercise the option is up to you. Whether your partner chooses to exercise their option is up to them.

Fenced, on the other hand, means that either you have agreed with your partner, explicitly or by default assumption, that it's not allowed or that (as in the case of swingers) permission is required beforehand.

Relationships go through phases. If you are in an unfenced relationship and you are, say, in the early romantic infatuation stage of your relationship, then you are probably not going to be interested at all in exercising your option. That's totally understandable and totally fine. So, just don't exercise your option.

The status of your relationship does not change from unfenced to fenced just because you are not interested in exercising your option right now. You are still in an unfenced relationship. You are just choosing not to exercise your option.

Seeing things in terms of fenced and unfenced gives us a better way to describe the dynamics of what is actually going on in sexual relationships, and so help us to clarify things and get our map closer to the terrain.

This then allows us to clear up a great deal of linguistic fog. For example, a one night stand is generally not regarded as a relationship. Indeed it is often talked about as the opposite of a relationship. But as discussed earlier, relationship simply means mutual reward.

When people find out a friend has found a new person and has hooked up with them, they often ask "a relationship or just a one night stand?" as if they are diametrically opposed.

The fact is that if both people got what they wanted – sex – then there was mutual reward. Therefore:

**Fog Alert**

*One night stand.*

This is often understood to be the opposite of a relationship.

A one night stand is a relationship.

It is an unfenced relationship of the duration of one night.

Now don't get me wrong--unfenced relationships do not just mean short term or casual relationships like one night stands, fuck buddies or friends with benefits.

Whether a relationship is fenced or unfenced has nothing at all to do with the level of affinity, love or pair bonding that may go on in either kind of relationship.

Thanks to relationship duress, it's a common assumption that a relationship not based on sexual ownership must be a casual and uncaring one, and that for a relationship to be a loving one, it must be fenced.

It's a totally false belief but an extremely prevalent one.

Society wants you to think exactly that, and employs an enormous amount of relationship duress to get you to do so.

It's tremendously important to society for you to keep this mapping error on your map.

In reality, the fenced world can provide you with a loveless marriage, and you can have an extremely loving and caring long term unfenced relationship.

So why does society need you to keep this mapping error on your map?

To answer that question, we have to go back to the beginning....

# 7 – Sex 1.0

## *Duration – All of human history until approximately 8,000 BC*

In order to understand the title of this book and what Sex 3.0 is, we first need to look at what Sex 1.0 and Sex 2.0 mean.

Without understanding the path that human sexual relationships took, and why we took this path, we cannot truly understand how and why we arrived at the present day situation. We need this understanding to have a good grasp of our future direction. Without it we cannot have a good map.

All of human history, when you include the species we evolved from, is an awfully long time. It is millions and millions of years, so let's just focus on the most relevant parts of the path that human sexuality has taken.

In this and the next few chapters, we are going to look at Sex 1.0, which is all of human history up until 10,000 years ago--or approximately 8,000 BC.

This means that in the last 200,000 years, Sex 1.0 is what we've had for about 95% of the time.

We spent pretty much all of the last 200,000 years living as hunter gathers.[v]

We roamed in small tribes of typically a dozen or two dozen people.[vi]

It was a nomadic existence, without permanent settlements, always moving to where food could be found, gathered and hunted. Wherever food, water and shelter were, that's where we had to go in order to survive.

During this time human beings had no concept of property.

This is the key to understanding Sex 1.0 – *no concept of property.*

Why? Well because property was not necessary for survival back then. In fact, bearing in mind how nomadic people were, and that you would need to carry with you any property you owned (which would slow you down), owning property would likely have *reduced* your chances of survival.

Without the concept of property, people cannot have self-interest--except in cases where survival resources were scarce and needed to be fought over.

In other words, the tribe would all look after each other. After a successful hunting and gathering foray, everybody in the tribe ate.

Hoarding food would have been regarded as shameful behaviour that could get you thrown out of the tribe. If that happened and you were left to fend for yourself, your chances of survival would plummet.

Behaviour that goes against tribal codes, or was disapproved of for any reason, could get you thrown out of the tribe. This fear of being left out on your own is the basis for why people conform.

This is what the Asch conformity experiments demonstrated so brilliantly--the instinctive desire of human beings to conform. It's an evolutionary desire that's still evident today.

This desire to conform developed during the Sex 1.0 period as a survival mechanism. It was a very useful form of fear at the time, to guard against the risk of getting thrown out of the tribe. Conformity was just part of our drive to survive.

# 8 – Nature's Desire

How many different animal species do you think exist in the world? Rabbits, giraffes, turtles, cats, penguins, dogs and so on....

According to what human science has been able to document, there are 8.7 million different animal species on the planet, of which we are one, and we all share nature's desire. [vii]

First of all, we all share nature's primary desire – the drive to survive!

This is the first thing nature demands of all of us, lest we share the fate of an estimated 99.9% of all species that have ever existed on planet Earth--which is, of course, extinction. [viii]

## The Primary Desire

If we break down nature's primary desire – survival – we see that it doesn't mean just to avoid death and remain alive. Survival also means genetic survival--the continuing existence of our DNA and of our own bloodline.

Survival also means protecting and looking after our children and grandchildren, ensuring that they too are well equipped to thrive and survive.

## The Two Primary Instincts

So as we said above, the primary desire breaks down into the two primary instincts, which are:

- Survival
- Reproduction

We can break down the two primary instincts even further, into the four basic needs.

## The Four Basic Needs

These are the only needs so basic that, if we humans as a species all stopped doing any one of the four, we would share the fate of the dodo and become extinct. They are:

- Eating
- Drinking
- Sleeping
- Fucking

We all stop eating? We all die.

We all stop drinking? We all die.

We all stop sleeping? The body collapses. We all die.

We all stop fucking? The human race would become extinct within one generation.

I am not saying these are the *only* things we need. What I am saying is that these are the only needs so basic that they are DNA-encoded, and that if we didn't follow them we would all be wiped out.

You might think you *need* your mobile phone but you don't. You ain't gonna die without it.

Nor am I saying these are all we need at the DNA level for survival and reproduction, but these are the only ones we need to concern ourselves with.

We need to breathe air but it's provided by the atmosphere. We need sunlight--the planet is just a big ice cube without it-- but we need not concern ourselves with procuring it because it's provided.

However, we do need to seek out food and drink when we're hungry and thirsty. We also need to find sexual partners, and we need to make sure we have a safe, warm, dry, comfortable place to bed down in order to sleep properly and be secure.

If it seems like I am stating the obvious here, you are right. Not only are these four needs obvious, but we can also see that your pet cat or dog or rabbit has exactly the same four basic needs.

This is worth noting, since many human beings think for reasons of ego that we are somehow above animals--that we are better than animals and above nature. If that's what you think, try an experiment. Don't eat or drink anything regardless of how hungry you are, and see how far it gets you.

Not only will you not have to deal with all of that nasty, animalistic expulsion of body waste, but you will soon be above nature and above animals altogether!

The reason for addressing something as obvious as the four basic needs is that it's interesting to look at differences in how human beings view and judge them.

Eating – If someone was hungry and ate food, would you judge them for it?

Drinking – If someone was thirsty and drank something, would you judge them for it?

Sleeping – If someone was tired and went for a nap, would you judge them for it?

Fucking – If someone was horny and had sex, would you judge them for it?

If your answer to the last question was different than your answer to the first three, ask yourself why.

The survival of the human race depends on all four, so we have powerful inborn drives for all of them. To stop doing any one of the four means the extinction of the species. So why judge sex?

Animals certainly would not judge any of the four needs---why do we?

Good question. It's not because we are "better" than animals. The answer lies in the evolution of human sexuality, and we will come to that in the next few chapters. But before we do, let's take a look at why sex even exists in the first place.

You might think you know, but the answer may surprise you.

# 9 – Why Does Sex Exist?

Why does sex exist?

If you are thinking "for fun," then you and I think alike and I raise a glass to you!

However, it's a serious question. If you do not know the answer to the question of why sex exists, then essentially you don't know why males and females exist, which means you can't know why you are a woman or why you are a man.

Looking at the question from a biological standpoint, the answer is quite surprising.

In the last chapter we talked about the two primary instincts – survival and reproduction. It must be one of those, right?

Yes, it's one of those so pick one. Biologically, does sex exist for survival or for reproduction?

Most people will say that sex exists for reproduction. This is where it gets interesting.

Anybody who took even basic biology at school knows that there is such a thing in nature as asexual reproduction--that is to say, creatures exist who don't need to have sex to reproduce. [ix]

Ok, human beings can't do asexual reproduction, but many frogs and worms can. Even large birds like turkeys can do it. The female turkey will, when isolated from male turkeys, begin to produce eggs by herself that are already fertilised. Many species can either reproduce asexually or can alternate between sexual and asexual reproduction as an adaption to their environment. [x]

Now, bearing in mind that Mother Nature knows this neat little trick of how to get a species to reproduce without sex--which demonstrates that sex is not necessary for reproduction in nature—we are left with a question.

If Mother Nature knows this trick, why would nature evolve most creatures, including ourselves of course, into male and female sexually reproducing creatures? Clearly it's not necessary in nature for reproduction, so why in us?

There must be some survival advantage to it because sexual reproduction, as compared to asexual reproduction, has many genetic survival *dis*advantages.

For example, unlike creatures that reproduce by cloning themselves, we have to go to all the trouble not only of searching for a mate, but also of competing for them too, perhaps even to the death.

If you are picturing nature documentary footage of peacocks going to all the effort of showing off their elaborate feathers, or male deer clashing antlers and fighting to the death on the African savannah, then you can imagine how easy the cloner's life is. Cloning is a feet-up-in-front-of-the-TV and calmly-enjoying-your-evening kind of existence, if ever there was one.

On top of that we might even contract a sexual transmitted disease as thanks for all our efforts. Thanks nature!

No nasty sexually transmitted diseases for the cloners, no need for violent competition with other members of your same species, and no need to ever leave the comfort of familiar and safe territory in the dangerous search for a mate across unknown terrain.

Wouldn't it be better if human beings reproduced asexually? Nightclubs across the world would be empty, churches would have to find something else to make people feel guilty about, and blues and soul musicians all around the world would have nothing to write songs about.

However, the impact would not all be positive, as we are about to find out.

The apparent genetic advantage of the cloners is something that has historically puzzled evolutionary biologists, but a compelling theory has emerged and been proven in lab conditions. I will talk about that theory here, as it may radically re-draw your map.

During asexual reproduction, animals produce an exact genetic copy of themselves--a clone. This makes sense, since their own DNA is the only DNA they have access to.

As mentioned earlier, female turkeys are capable of producing fertilised eggs on their own if they're kept isolated from male turkeys. But the chicks produced asexually will not be as physically strong, and are more likely to succumb to disease.

The answer to the question of whether sex exists for survival or for reproduction therefore rests with genetic diversity.

When reproduction happens sexually, 50% of the DNA of the father gets thrown away, as does 50% of the DNA of the mother. The offspring gets the rest.

Except in cases of identical twins (or triplets, etc.) the offspring won't get the same 50% each time, which is why siblings of the same sex born to the same parents even one year apart don't look exactly alike, even though they share almost all the same genes.

In a cloned species however, offspring are exact genetic copies.

So what happens if a parasite is introduced into the environment of a clone?

If the parasite is successful at attacking and killing even one clone in that environment, and then the parasite spreads to other members of the species, how successful is the parasite going to be?

Clearly a successful parasite can easily wipe out an entire species without ever having to change or evolve to deal with different genetic signatures.

In sexually-reproducing species however, the constant mixing and rearranging of genetic signatures helps the species stay a step ahead of parasites, making it very difficult for any parasite to wipe out an entire species.

This constant DNA reshuffling gives newborn babies genetic signatures that are potentially better at dealing with parasites that their parents grew up with, which is a huge advantage in this evolutionary and biological arms race. [xi]

Therefore, sex exists in nature for reasons of survival – not reproduction.

So applying pure form theory to the question of why sex exists, we can answer in just one or two words – "parasite defence" or "biodiversity." [xii]

It gives a new perspective to realise that the reason you *are* a woman or a man is due to the requirement for a parasite defence mechanism.

This is why both sexes exist in beautiful symbiosis. Both sexes help to ensure the survival of the other and of human race.

It seems that, if you really enjoy sex, you have a lot to thank those pesky parasites for.

# 10 – Why Men and Women Don't Understand Each Other

There is one thing more than anything else that explains all male and female emotional and behavioural differences.

Since we are still in the Sex 1.0 section of the book, I will talk in this chapter about how this one thing worked in the Sex 1.0 era, but its impact on the present day will become clear later in the chapter.

When you get to the Sex 2.0 section, I will talk at that point about how the shift from Sex 1.0 to Sex 2.0 somewhat changed this one thing.

Without knowing about this one thing, or if you know but later forget it when re-drawing your map, you might end up thinking that men and women seem to be from different planets.

But we are not. Men are not from Mars and women are not from Venus. Men are from Earth, women are from Earth.

So what is this one thing?

## The Genetic Imperative

When I say "genetic imperative" I simply mean the most efficient method possible for propagating one's own DNA--or, the most efficient biological self-preservation strategy.

Since men and women are biologically different, we developed radically different genetic imperatives.

Once pregnant, and assuming the pregnancy goes to full term, women cannot produce another viable egg for approximately 9-10 months.

Men, however, can produce sperm constantly, pausing only for what is called the refractory period (the recovery phase after male ejaculation, during which it is physiologically impossible for a man to further ejaculate).

Women have no such refractory period, and can often achieve further orgasms through further stimulation.

As men can produce sperm fairly constantly, and women have a minimum 9-10 month pause before they become fertile again (during which time they are physically more vulnerable, less mobile and require more care), the genetic imperatives for the sexes are radically different. Their development in the Sex 1.0 world was like this:

Men = Have sex with lots of fertile females

Women = Seek high quality alpha male DNA, and physical protection and security for both self and child.

The genetic imperative is not peculiar to human beings. Mammals in general--where the female gestates the egg for months and males can constantly produce sperm--have the same genetic imperative.

The female need for security and protection is of course heightened by the child-rearing responsibility, for which women historically have carried the burden.

## Sizing the Prize

One of the things that humans share with all sexual species is that we "size the prize."

That is to say that people not only size up potential mates according to how well they might be able to satisfy their genetic imperatives, but we also size up ourselves and our own value in the sexual marketplace.

The differing genetic imperatives in the Sex 1.0 era meant that men and women were naturally attracted by different things in a Sex 1.0 world, and these differences have influenced the course of human sexual history.

Men value signs of fertility and physical attractiveness in women--such as youth, beauty and curves in all the right places.

Women, on the other hand, value alpha genes as well as the best provision of security for self and child.

These differing values made men and women naturally seek different things.

Broadly speaking, the differing genetic imperatives dictated that men have always sought to entice women into sex, and that women have always sought to entice men into commitment.

## The Alpha Male

Social animals like human beings have always had higher- and lower-ranking members in any particular social group or tribe.

The alpha male in a Sex 1.0 world would have been a leader. He would have been strong, capable and skilled at hunting and gathering. He would have been capable of providing and protecting. He would have been respected by the other members of the tribe, which is why "social proof" is something that, even today, women find very attractive.

Other attractive and alpha qualities are pre-selection. There is nothing more desirable to women than a man that other women desire.

Alpha males are, by their very nature, dominant.

## The Beta Male

The beta male would have been lacking in strength, leadership qualities, social proof and pre-selection.

He would have been too weak or scared to challenge the dominance of the alpha male.

Beta males are, by their very nature, pussies.

## Men are from Earth, Women are from Earth

The differing genetic imperatives cause not only unhealthy thinking—like that men and women are from different planets—but it also causes all kinds of "I don't get it" moments for both men and women.

These "I don't get it" moments about the opposite sex are often due to lack of understanding about the differing genetic imperatives at work--not just in the opposite sex, but in oneself.

For example, men typically love competitive sports, both playing and watching, and might spend a great deal of time during their lives supporting their favourite teams.

Sports stadiums around the world are filled with both men and women, but as you and I both know, it's mostly men.

Plenty of women I have spoken to say that they don't "see the point" of things like football, that they don't "get it," nor do they understand that they are actually the root cause of it.

Women tend to be totally unaware that the very existence of competitive sports is a direct result of the female genetic imperative.

The female genetic imperative dictates that the alpha (i.e. the man or men in the tribe who are the leaders, the best, the most dominant, the winners) are sexually desirable. They are the men that women were attracted to and sought in a Sex 1.0 world.

The winner is seen as the "last man standing," which is obviously a desirable quality for a woman seeking to satisfy her genetic imperative not only to be protected, but for her children to have good survival genes. This imperative is still demonstrably operative in women in the modern day.

I have personally witnessed women going into a state of awe-struck fandom when famous football players are spotted in a nightclub. They have immediately phoned their female friends with the news, giving instructions to immediately come and join them--even though these exact same women "don't see the point" of football, and are not inclined either to go to or to watch games.

Some men "don't get" this.

Women swooning over football players whilst having no interest in football itself is very easy to understand when you get that to physically compete and dominate is not generally part of the female psycho-sexual landscape, but that attraction to the alpha male very much *is*.

The only competition that is generally part of the female psycho-sexual landscape is competing with other women over the alpha, and this is the root cause of female-on-female cattiness and bitchiness. Female competition is why women often call each other "slag" or "tramp" or some other derisory term in relation to an alpha male.

As a result of "the winners" being desired by women, men quite rightly have always derived great enjoyment from all kinds of sporting competitions and battles of dominance.

It's a guy thing.

Another example is the World Series of Poker (every year in Las Vegas), in which the (mostly male) poker commentators wring their hands and bemoan the fact that such a small percentage of entrants into the competition are female.

They don't get it.

After all, the poker competition is open to everyone. They ponder what can be done to make poker more attractive to women.

What can be done? Well, the solution would be to change the genetic imperative and completely rewrite human nature. Good luck with that.

Another example is that video game designers (again, mostly male) have historically struggled to design video games that appeal to women. Why are women not so interested in blowing stuff up and beating up or killing off opponent's characters as men are?

They don't get it.

Woman enjoy overcoming challenges every bit as much as men do, but they are generally not interested in dominating and destroying as much as men are, so it's not a coincidence that the most popular video games for women are games like the following :

- Tetris—a puzzle game which does not involve dominating and defeating an opponent.

- World of Warcraft—a game in which people form tightly knit guilds or social groups, forge human interactions, and work cooperatively on common goals, missions and objectives, thereby overcoming challenges together.

• Wii Fit – A game that makes exercise fun and helps keep them looking and feeling good. Helps them get or maintain signs of youth and beauty.

• Guitar Hero/Rock Band type games, in which you can play together with your friends in a party atmosphere and co-operate on "playing" songs well and working as a team to make the band a success.

Whilst on the subject of video games, it's interesting to note that men who play a lot of video games are typified as nerdy and beta.

Alpha men enjoy video games just as much as beta men do, but I believe the reason beta males are more drawn to video games is that they allow them to indulge in alpha-type dominance in a completely safe environment, sheltered from the real world. Often betas will do so as a way of consoling and comforting themselves over real-world failures:

"Ok--so I may be 34 years old, live in my mom's basement and don't have a girlfriend, but my level 15 warlock will destroy you on the internet!!"

Of course, even though alphas really enjoy video games too, they get less free time to play them because they are busy having sex.

In summary, men and women don't "get" each other in many cases as a result of not understanding the differing genetic imperatives, or because they project the imperative of their own sex onto the opposite sex.

Later in this book we will see examples of how this impacts modern-day sexual relationships.

# 11 – The Sex 1.0 Marketplace

As mentioned earlier, during the Sex 1.0 era human beings lived in nomadic tribes and had no concept of property.

That fact does not mean that people did not compete for survival resources.

## Competition and Territory

All creatures follow nature's primary desire, which is survival. This means that all animals will compete when they need to, for reasons of scarcity or any other reasons, over survival resources like food and mating opportunities.

An *extremely* common mapping mistake is to confuse competition over territory and survival resources in other creatures with the uniquely human notion of property.

If you put ten animals of any species in a confined space and provide only enough food for two of them, the animals will fight over it--not because they think the food is their property, but just because they have to in order to survive. They have no choice but to fight. Likewise, all animals compete over mating opportunities if they need to.

Competition for survival resources should not be confused with concepts of property.

Being "territorial" should not be confused with property either. Being territorial simply means defending the space immediately around you, wherever that happens to be, and defending the survival resources within it.

A hunter-gatherer could be territorial in one space, and could move five miles the next day and be territorial about that space also, whilst completely forgetting the space he was territorial about the day before. Property had no meaning and therefore did not exist.

What does this have to do with sex? Everything.

If you have no concept of property, then human beings cannot be sexual property.

Therefore, there was no marriage in Sex 1.0. And since there was no concept of marriage, there was also no concept of boyfriend/girlfriend relationships in the conventional sense, since those are essentially try-before-you-buy arrangements with the intention that they should lead to marriage.

As a species, we quite simply just followed our sexual nature. In this respect we were exactly the same as the other 8.7 million species on the planet.

In other words, *all* sexual relationships in a Sex 1.0 world were unfenced.

Men and women hunted and gathered and were pretty much equal in a socio-economic sense. Nobody was "rich," because there was no concept of money or property. Children were raised collaboratively by the tribe.

People, both men and women, simply competed in the sexual marketplace for what they both wanted and needed in order to satisfy their respective biological imperatives.

Females used their youth and their fertility to attract the best alpha males.

Alpha males used their alpha-ness, their desirable qualities like leadership, strength, dominance, good hunting and gathering skills and so on to attract the most fertile and attractive females.

## The Spectrum Dilemma

Alpha males dominated the Sex 1.0 marketplace, meaning they dominated the opportunities for mating with the fertile females. The beta males were left out in the cold in that respect and got very little or no action. They lived a largely sexless life, and the most they could hope for was to survive. Survival was not best achieved by challenging the alpha-male dominance, because that might lead to a beating or to death.

This made for an interesting dynamic that is still at play today, which is alpha and beta males living in essentially two different realities, even though they may be in the same social group.

For the alpha male, the reality was that women were attracted to and available to him. An alpha's mentality would be one of sexual abundance, and the best way for a woman to be especially desirable to him was to have signs of youth and fertility.

Beta males, on the other hand, lived with a scarcity mentality, in which they would take whatever they could get.

This is why men even today have a crushing fear of rejection and are scared to approach women--and perhaps might never do so without the Dutch courage that a few drinks can provide.

This is also why the more desirable the woman, the greater the fear. Logically, experiencing greater fear because a woman is more superficially beautiful makes no sense at all, if you bear in mind that all women have the same sex organs and that the male genetic imperative is to have sex with lots of women.

But this fear is totally understandable, since being rejected by a woman with fewer signs of attractiveness and fertility would be regarded as less of a slight (in terms of pre-selection and social proof amongst a small tribe of people) than would be the crushing rejection from a more obviously fertile and desirable woman. Also, the knowledge that a more attractive woman is far more likely to be sought by alphas drastically heightens male fear, since conflict with an alpha over a survival resource could mean death.

The spectrum dilemma for a beta male in the Sex 1.0 era always meant that his lack of success guaranteed even less success in the future. Women don't want a guy who is low in the social hierarchy and unwanted by other women.

The spectrum dilemma works in reverse for an alpha. Receiving pre-selection from other women as well as social proof from the tribe in general would have made him even more highly desirable.

The spectrum dilemma at play in the Sex 1.0 marketplace would have had a clearly polarising effect for men, shoving them to either one end of the spectrum or the other, and leaving very little in the middle.

Beta males in the Sex 1.0 marketplace mostly got weeded out of the genetic pool. Their genetic survival chances were poor, whilst alphas' genes thrived.

## The Big Shift

The shift from Sex 1.0 to Sex 2.0 started about 8,000 BC, during the neolithic era. Humanity started to go through the agricultural revolution, also known as the neolithic revolution.[xiii]

People began to move away from the nomadic hunter-gatherer way of life, and started to rely on agriculture and farming. This allowed us to live in settlements for the first time in human history; to have towns and villages; and to live a settled lifestyle.

Relying for survival on food that we *grew* led human beings to develop, for the first time, the notion of property.

The first property that ever existed was land--specifically fertile land that was good for farming.

Land itself was never scarce, and since the world's population was much lower back then (less than one person per square mile), there would be no reason to covet or own land, especially if it was rocky or barren.

However, land that was good for growing food *was* scarce, and so for the first time ever in human history we cared about owning property.

The invention of property changed *everything,* and was the catalyst for the transition from Sex 1.0 to Sex 2.0.

# 12 – The Birth of Sex 2.0

***Duration – 8,000 BC until the present day***

Of the 8.7 million species of animals on the planet, we are the only one that has any concept of property. Dolphins don't own shit, and it's not because they are stupid and we are intelligent. Dolphins are intelligent creatures.

Once human beings developed the concept of property, we became unique on the planet but not necessarily in a good way.

The first impact on human sexuality was that it became very important for men to treat women as sexual property. The reason behind this is simple. Ownership of property such as fertile land, farm animals, a house and other survival resources comes along with the desire to pass these on.

So why would women and not men become sexual property?

Well, regardless of what culture or ethnicity you grow up in, which language you speak, or what region of the world you are from, one thing never changes. When a newborn baby arrives, it comes out of the body of a woman and not of a man.

That means a woman does not need to worry about the possibility that she might be raising somebody else's child. It came out of her body, so it's self-evident that it's her child.

No matter how many men the woman has had sex with, she knows for a fact that she is the mother even though she may or may not know who the father is.

Men do not have that luxury.

A woman knows that all of the time and emotional and financial effort she puts toward that child is an investment in the survival of her own bloodline, whereas men do not have that luxury.

Men experience paternity concern (or PAC for short) – the worry that they may be raising somebody else's child, passing their survival resources (property) down somebody else's blood line and not their own and best ensuring the survival of somebody else's children.

Women cannot experience maternity concern because the self-evident nature of childbirth means they are left in no doubt as to the identity of the mother.

In the Sex 1.0 era, paternity concern was never really an issue of much concern. During practically all of the Sex 1.0 era, calendars had not yet been invented. Without calendars, it is fantastically unlikely that people would have been aware that there was any connection at all between having sex and, roughly 270 sunrises later, a baby arriving.

They would have assumed that the same pagan or shamanic gods that governed the tides and the rains placed the baby inside the woman (a belief that led to the rise of the notion of the virgin birth, which later became a popular motif in many religions).

Also, with no concept of property in Sex 1.0--meaning no property-based self-interest, no material goods to pass down, and all children being raised and looked after by the tribe as a whole--paternity concern was not so important.

The invention of property changed everything.

During the conception and birth of Sex 2.0, if paternity concern was the sperm, then the egg was the invention of property.

No creature, human or otherwise, acts against their nature unless they have a reason to.

But the invention of property when mixed with paternity concern formed a combination so powerful that it gave us a reason to act against our nature. That mixture was the potent catalyst in moving humanity from Sex 1.0 to Sex 2.0.

In order to deal with the paternity concern that men now had (as a result of the role that property now played in the survival of their bloodline), a new deal had to be struck.

A deal was sought that would ease male insecurity, ensure the paternity of their children, perpetuate their own genes and pass property down their own bloodline.

The deal had to allow men to claim women as their sexual property—i.e. to demand women's fidelity in order to allay paternity concern.

So what was the deal?

# 13 – Marriage, the Sex 2.0 Deal

Marriage was invented during the neolithic era to address these very problems.[xiv]

The written word in human history did not begin to appear until approximately 3,200 BC, so the first marriages likely pre-date written human records by thousands of years.[xv] These marriages would probably have been verbally-bartered agreements whereby a man provided care, security and access to survival resources to a woman, in exchange for exclusive sexual access.

This would allow him to calm his PAC, thereby assuring that his genetic legacy was safe, as was the passing down of survival resources to his own children rather than to anyone else's.

No specific civil ceremonies were likely required. And since the Neolithic era pre-dates the main modern religions – Christianity, Judaism and Islam - by thousands of years, there were no religious ceremonies either; at least none that resembled a modern religious ceremony.[xvi]

The origin of marriage has nothing at all to do with religion. This might come as a surprise, since in modern-day society marriage and religion are thought to be closely connected.[xvii]

The religions that existed at the time marriage was invented were shamanic religions, or the pagan religions of the Greeks, Romans and Egyptians. However, the modern religions that came later had to adopt certain pagan or shamanic traditions in order to successfully attract converts.[xviii] [xix]

Although people started to strike marriage-like deals thousands and thousands of years ago, they continue to the present day and form the heart of the Sex 2.0 deal.

## *The Sex 2.0 Deal*

We all live in a Sex 2.0 society today.

When you are raised in a Sex 2.0 society, men and women are taught to believe in what I call the Sex 2.0 deal. There are two sides to this deal, the male side and the female side.

Women are raised and taught their entire life that they have to sell their sexuality in exchange for security--ultimately the security of marriage to a man.

Men are raised and taught their entire life that if you want to have a long term sexual relationship with a woman, you have to take her sexuality, throw it in a box, slam the lid shut and stamp and label the box as their property.

So:

Men – You have to make a woman's sexuality your property to deal with paternity concern (PAC) and best ensure that you are raising your own kids, and you have to provide both wife and kids with security. In return …

Women – You have to sell your exclusive sexuality to a man in exchange for security.

Women who don't follow the Sex 2.0 deal are widely insulted, derided and made to feel cheap and worthless, not just by men but by women too, amazingly enough. We cover this in more detail later in the book.

In many cultures, men who don't follow the Sex 2.0 deal are not considered men. They are not considered men until they are married. I remember when I was travelling Vietnam a local man told me that, regardless of how old you are, you are not considered a real man in Vietnamese culture until you are married. So a married 19-year-old is considered a man there, and an unmarried 29-year-old is not.

The pressures and enforced obligations placed on us by society are prevalent forms of relationship duress.

As a result of the Sex 2.0 deal, something very interesting happened.

At the point in human sexual history when that deal was struck, a schism was created. And although that time was thousands and thousands of years ago, the schism persists to the present day.

This schism is right now the predominant cause of almost all of the confusion and suffering in modern-day sexual relationships around the entire world.

# 14 – The Root Cause of Our Problems

In the Sex 1.0 era, human sexuality operated on only one plane (or dimension if you prefer), defined by the word "natural."

Like all of the other 8.7 million species of creatures occupying this beautiful planet, we lived in harmony with our sexual nature.

Then something happened, and lots of things changed.

To understand it, visualise a drinks coaster on the table in front of you.

If you actually have one, place it to your left hand side. If you don't have one, then just imagine it there or use something else, like a glass, cup, or whatever.

This represents a plane of human sexuality that is *natural.* In Sex 1.0 this kind of sexuality is all we had and all we needed.

```
┌─────────────────┐
│                 │
│                 │
│     Natural     │
│                 │
│                 │
└─────────────────┘
```

Back then we operated sexually just like every other species on the planet; we just followed our sexual nature.

We shook nature by the hand, smiled and went along with it. Sure, we competed and even fought in times of scarcity, but we were in tune with nature.

However, when we moved from Sex 1.0 to Sex 2.0, a fundamental schism was created, and this split meant that human sexually began to operate on *two planes at the same time.*

Now picture or place another drinks coaster in front of you and over to your right hand side.

This represents the newly-introduced plane of human sexuality in Sex 2.0, which is defined by the word "normal."

*The Sex 2.0 Schism*

So you now have one on your left and one on your right, representing the two planes of human sexuality in a Sex 2.0 world. The one on the left is the "natural" sexual plane and the one on the right is the "normal" sexual plane.

The word natural simply means "in accord (or agreement) with nature." It does not mean anything else. Natural is defined by nature alone and is not defined by society.

The word "normal," on the other hand, is defined by society as what's expected or what "everyone" does. Probably you already have a gut sense of what "societal norm" means.

This is an important distinction, and worth repeating.

**Natural = defined by nature and not by society**

## Normal = defined by society and not by nature

The Sex 2.0 era was the first time in human history when it became possible to have something that is completely 100% normal, and is at the same time totally unnatural.
Hmmmmm...........like marriage, for example.

Marriage is totally normal but it is also completely unnatural Human beings are not by nature monogamous *for life*, whereas marriage requires you to promise exactly that.

Widespread adoption of a practice does not make it any more natural; it just makes it more normal.

Marriage is completely normal, and you have likely lived your entire life in a society where marriage is not only considered the norm, but is expected of you under relationship duress.

The shift from Sex 1.0 to Sex 2.0 did not change the underlying nature of human sexuality at all. We did not suddenly change to become sexually monogamous for life--we were just expected to behave that way.

The shift to Sex 2.0 also did not change the physical act of sex at all. It simply changed what society expected and insisted on as acceptable for sexual long term relationships.

This simple change, however, created the amazing shift from operating in accord with our nature--as every other species on the planet still does today—to going against our nature, under relationship duress.

The split from operating on one sexual plane – the natural – to two sexual planes at the same time – natural and normal – is the root cause of pretty much all of the confusion in modern human sexuality.

Once the normal sexual plane was introduced, something interesting happened and something interesting did not happen.

What *did* happen is that relationship duress was introduced to cajole, pressure and otherwise obligate and force people to choose the normal plane.

What did *not* happen is that human sexual nature did not change, not even one tiny little bit.

Contrary to the popular saying, repeating a lie often enough does not make it the truth.

# 15 – The Sex 2.0 Genetic Imperative

The genetic imperative for men and women has always simply been about the most efficient and effective gateway to genetic immortality, via the survival of one's immediate descendants. This continued to be so in a Sex 2.0 world.

Since women are the ones who get pregnant, their most successful genetic strategy in a Sex 1.0 era was to seek superior genes and alpha males for protection. By doing both, women best ensured their own and their children's survival.

Since men don't go through the nine-month gestation period, and can produce sperm constantly, their imperative was always to seek various fertile women and have as much sex with them as possible.

The arrival of the Sex 2.0 era somewhat changed and somewhat didn't change the genetic imperative.

In a Sex 1.0 world women, like men, had only one genetic imperative.

Women = Seek high quality alpha male DNA and physical protection and security for both self and child.

Men = Have sex with lots of fertile females

In a Sex 1.0 world, with no concept of property or money, nobody was rich or poor. There *was* a social hierarchy, but it consisted of alphas and betas, and of youth and beauty or their lack. There was no financial hierarchy.

Once the concept of property, and later on the related concept of money, was introduced, it was inevitable that some people became richer than others. They made better farms or farming tools than others and acquired wealth that way, or they provided better goods and services.

Others did not have jobs but became wealthy simply because they owned the means of production or gained wealth from being influential in decision-making and granting monopolies. In other words, they became politicians.

For the first time in human history, we had an economic elite.

If you married into such a family, then your children would most likely be born into an abundance of financial survival resources.

The move from having just a social class to having both a social *and* an economic class in a Sex 2.0 world meant that women--but not men--gained an extra genetic imperative.

Women's survival strategy altered, and now there were two primary considerations that a woman had to take into account to ensure her best DNA survival strategy.

The female imperative changed from:

> 1 - Seek high quality alpha male DNA and physical protection and security for both self and child (socio)

The female imperative changed to:

> 1 - Seek high quality alpha male DNA and physical protection and security for both self and child (socio)
>
> 2 - Seek a partner who can provide financial security for self and children. Prevent other women from diluting such arrangement (economic).

We moved from a socio world to a socio-economic world.

Since women in the Sex 2.0 era – the last 10,000 years - have largely carried the overwhelming burden of childcare and raising children, this second biological imperative is unique to them.

Men's biological imperative did not change at all, and it still dictates that men's genetically most successful strategy is to have sex with lots of fertile women.

The creation of the second female imperative introduced "hypergamy" into the mix, which means essentially "marrying up," or seeking a sexual-exclusivity-in-exchange-for-security contract with a man of high standing. [xx]

This could simply be a man who is richer, more powerful and more socially influential than she is, or, in the Indian sub-continent, marrying into a higher caste.

However, a woman does not necessarily need to get both genetic imperatives met by the same man, and women often don't. Marrying the beta provider/millionaire and banging the alpha male yoga instructor or ex-boyfriend is extremely common.

This change in the female sexual imperatives had a radical effect on what was to become the Sex 2.0 marketplace.

# 16 – The Sex 2.0 Marketplace

The revolution that brought the Sex 2.0 marketplace into existence was an interesting one.

With Sex 1.0, everyone was equally "poor," and the marketplace was simply a competition for mating opportunities. The competition that existed was about fertility in women and alphaness in men.

Broadly speaking, men's role was to entice women into sex, and women's role was to entice men into commitment.

Relationships typically lasted as long as the pair bond between the couple lasted, which nature ensured was enough time to see a vulnerable child and mother through the first few years.[xxi]

## Goodbye Sex 1.0, Hello Sex 2.0

As we've seen, property combined with paternity concern (PAC) was the catalyst for the seismic shift from Sex 1.0 to 2.0.

The defining feature of all sexual relationships in Sex 2.0 is that they are based on the concept of sexual ownership.

Ownership creates a drastically different sexual marketplace.

Sex 1.0 meant all relationships were unfenced. Sex 2.0 means relationships are fenced (i.e. based on sexual ownership and exclusive sexual access).

Sex 1.0 meant competition in the sexual marketplace was solely socio-based (i.e. fertility/alpha). Sex 2.0 means competition in the sexual marketplace is socio-economic.

Sex 1.0 meant no relationship duress. Sex 2.0 requires the entire system to be heavily enforced by relationship duress, along with its insistence on the standard script of dating -> marriage (or arranged marriage).

Under Sex 2.0, marriage and the nuclear family unit became the means whereby wealth and genes were mixed together and perpetuated. Economic differentiation meant that marriage became the vehicle for transmitting status and property as well as a best practice for establishing genetic lineage.

Therefore, being in a Sex 2.0 society as we all are, you have grown up with false information and relationship duress, which insist there are only two choices when it comes to long term sexual relationships.

1 - Boyfriend/Girlfriend

2 - Husband/Wife

In many conservative countries, even boyfriend/girlfriend is not endorsed by society. Sex before marriage is either not allowed or is frowned upon.

Even in western societies today, boyfriend/girlfriend sexual relationships are not actively celebrated by society at large.

If you have a boyfriend/girlfriend sexual relationship, nobody is going to slap you on the back, congratulate you, break out the cigars, give you a big cake and lots of presents, and organise an expensive party for you.

Nooooooooo. Boyfriend/girlfriend relationships are tolerated as a "try before you buy" deal, in the hope that the sale is made.

When the sale is made, *then* we will slap you on the back, congratulate you, break out the cigars, give you a big cake and lots of presents, and organise an expensive party for you.

Hey, we will even throw confetti at you!

Speaking of which …

# 17 – Why Marriage is Not Natural

Ladies and gents, we have been outvoted! There are 8.7 million different species of animal on the planet. We are the only species on the planet that gets married.

This means that we have been outvoted on the question of whether marriage is natural or not by roughly 8,700,000 to 1.

We are not getting married because we are so special or smart or so much better. If you believe that then you are a walking, talking testament to the narcissism of human beings.

Inventing a system by which we can go against nature, and then creating a society in which people are obliged to choose it even though the new system is seriously and very obviously flawed, does not make us smart.

One could argue the opposite. The fact that dolphins don't waste their time and squander precious survival resources on expensive lawyers in divorce courts does not make dolphins dumber than we are.

Beyond that, the argument that marriage is natural is a totally self-defeating one. If marriage were natural, people would follow this sequence, with no outside influence or coercion whatsoever:

Boy meets girl -> boy and girl hook-up -> boy and girl stay together in lifelong monogamy

You see the problem? If this was the *natural* sequence, there would be no need whatsoever to invent marriage in order to allay paternity concern.

If this was the natural sequence, the word *marriage* would not exist and the concept of marriage would never have been invented. There would simply be no need for it.

It is precisely because this is *not* the natural sequence that marriage had to be invented.

Monogamy for life goes against human nature. This was very well understood at the dawn of property, which is why something had to be invented to enforce it and the Sex 2.0 deal.

Even the church, in the marriage vows themselves, implicitly acknowledges the fact that monogamy is unnatural and that people need sexual variety. Why else would the vows specify "forsaking all others 'til death do you part?"

If monogamy were natural, there would be zero need for a vow NOT to do something that you are never going to have any interest in or desire to do anyway.

If marriage vows are going to be about NOT doing stuff that you're never going to do anyway, go wild! You may as well forsake your right to wander down the local high street naked except for a false beard made of the finest horse hair, painted blue whilst playing the banjo.

The vow to "forsake all others" is the church's tacit acknowledgement that you're going to want to be unfenced. It's saying, "But don't! You have to promise not to! But no seriously, at some point during the marriage you are definitely going to want to do that—maybe with that person at work who has been flirting with you--a few drinks after work and you are seriously going to want to. But don't! It will make god angry!"

Marriage is totally normal, and it is also completely unnatural.

Earlier in the book I explained that there are only two kinds of relationship – fenced and unfenced.

Also, you might recall that I mentioned you can have a fenced relationship that is not monogamous (like a married couple who are swingers), and that you can have an unfenced relationship that is monogamous (i.e. you choose not to exercise your sexual options).

This gives a clear distinction between fenced and unfenced, and also a clear distinction as to why fenced and unfenced are *not* synonymous with monogamy and polygamy.

Think back to the drinks coasters representing the two planes of human sexuality--natural and normal.

Although fenced and unfenced relationships are *not* synonymous with monogamy and polygamy, they *are* synonymous with the two planes of human sexuality.

Fenced relationships are synonymous with the "normal" plane, and unfenced relationships are synonymous with the "natural" plane. Hence, in Sex 2.0, the normal sexual plane is where fenced sexual relationships belong and the natural sexual plane is where unfenced sexual relationships belong.

You can think of fenced and unfenced as the flip sides of normal and natural coasters. Since this book is 2D and not 3D though, they look like this:

```
┌─────────────┐          ┌─────────────┐
│             │          │             │
│  Natural /  │          │  Normal /   │
│  Unfenced   │          │  Fenced     │
│             │          │             │
└─────────────┘          └─────────────┘
```

The use of relationship duress in a Sex 2.0 world means that these two options are not presented to you with a discussion of the relative merits of each.

No, no, no!

Society shoves the normal sexual plane in your face your whole life, telling you "Choose this! Choose this! You have to choose this!"

Under Sex 2.0, human sexual nature became marginalised.

That's what relationship duress is for.

# 18 – Relationship Duress

Fenced relationships were not the only thing that arrived at the dawn of the Sex 2.0 marketplace.

Relationship duress also arrived, in order to pressure people into fenced relationships.

What is relationship duress? Well, imagine somebody pulled a gun on you and said "You and me are gonna rob a bank. If you don't come rob the bank with me I'll kill you. If you come to the bank with me but panic and run away, I know where your family lives and I'm gonna kill them." You'd probably go rob the bank.

When you got caught by the police you might tell them, "Yes I committed the crime, but I did so under duress. He had a gun to my head so I didn't have a choice."

Both men and women in a Sex 2.0 world are raised to believe that, in order to have a loving, pair-bonded, long term sexual relationship, it has to be fenced. You don't have a choice.

I call bullshit on that one. That's just a form of relationship duress which society burdens you with.

Society says that the Sex 2.0 deal and its insistence on fenced relationships is so wonderfully, amazingly desirable for both parties that if you don't choose it there must be something terribly wrong with you.

This brings us to the crux of the matter. If the Sex 2.0 deal is so wonderfully desirable, then why would any kind of force or duress be required to get us to choose it?

If the deal is so great, why employ even the tiniest bit of pressure? Why would that be necessary?

The reason relationship duress is necessary is precisely because fenced relationships are not natural.

Think about it. If fenced relationships were natural, then they would be chosen by everybody anyway, therefore removing the need for relationship duress.

Another form of relationship duress is that the natural option of unfenced relationships is never even offered. Sex 2.0 society keeps that hidden and obscured. We like to pretend that it just doesn't exist, so we keep it covered up.

If you realise that natural sexuality is an option and choose it from the very beginning of a relationship, society comes out with all kinds of Sex 2.0 relationship duress nonsense like "Well that's not a real relationship," or "You must be just fuck buddies or just friends with benefits," and other ways to label your choice as illegitimate.

It's laughable that, in the year that this book was written, not one but two Hollywood movies have been written with identical plotlines about couples who attempt unfenced relationships. Of course in both movies the couples decide that the only *possible* way to go about this is not to be caring, pair bonded and loving towards each other--just sex, no emotion.

### Fog Alert

*Fuck buddies/Friends with benefits*

These terms do not mean unfenced relationships. They mean relationships that are not loving or pair bonded.

It is entirely possible to having loving relationships without sexual ownership and without the crushing pressures of jealousy and possessiveness. Just don't expect to see that in a Hollywood rom-com any time soon.

I painfully sat through both movies for research reasons and watched how Natalie Portman joined the ranks of actresses waving the flag for Sex 2.0 relationship duress. Natalie, shame on you! You too, Mila!

Justin Timberlake, I am disappointed. Aston Kutcher, I am really not surprised.

Interestingly, Kutcher's marriage collapsed later the same year the movie was released. He attributed the collapse to the fact that "Marriage is one of the hardest things in the world," without elaborating about why this is so.

(Ok, so I'll cut him a break. He said that in a twitter message, where there isn't much room to elaborate even if he could.)

In Sex 2.0, relationship duress becomes necessary as an additional "insurance policy" because the Sex 2.0 deal by itself does not guarantee the elements it seeks to guarantee, which are:

> 1 - The paternity of the children of the male involved in the deal, for the passing down of property to his bloodline
>
> 2 - The eradication of paternity *concern*
>
> 3 - The perpetuation of the genes of the male involved

Even if both parties getting married swear in a religious ceremony to forsake all others, this still does not guarantee anything. It's only the best attempt to ensure it.

A vow of fidelity is a promise, not a guarantee.

This is the case even in countries where women are not allowed to leave the house unless accompanied by a close male relative and dressed from head to toe in garments that hide their body. No guarantee exists even given the fact that children often bear a genetic resemblance to their father, because the other men that have access to her may be close genetic relations of her husband.

So because there are no guarantees, there needed to be the additional insurance policy of relationship duress.

## The Many Faces of RD

Relationship duress (RD) comes in many forms. For example, celebrities like Tiger Woods, John Terry etc. have to pretend in the spotlight that they are role models in their love lives-- when they are just as human as the rest of us.

Or divorce. When you choose divorce or divorce is chosen for you by your partner, there is still a wall you have to face. The divorce process itself can be long, drawn out, expensive and socially and financially very difficult and damaging. These hardships are all forms of relationship duress.[xxii]

One of the things I was frequently asked by people I interviewed during my two-plus years of travelling, writing and researching this book was, "What are the big differences and similarities across cultures when it comes to sexual relationships?"

The answer is that the societal agenda of promoting fenced relationships is the same all over the world. It is universal, not because, as so many people believe, it is a high-functioning system that guarantees happiness. It's universal because only women give birth regardless of what country you are from, and because the concept of property is universal.

So travelling from one country to another, the agenda does not change. What does change is the level of RD, intimidation and violence, particularly directed toward women, that is used to maintain the agenda.

To repeat: the fenced relationship agenda is global.

In low RD countries people are more sexually liberal, and there's a lower level of obligation, violence and intimidation. In high RD countries people are more sexually conservative, and these levels are higher.

Turkey is an interesting case study since it's where the mostly lower-RD countries of Europe intersect with the mostly higher-RD countries of the Middle East.

In western Turkish cities like Istanbul there is nothing shocking about unmarried couples walking hand-in-hand down the street, and although sex before marriage is frowned on, it's largely accepted or at least tolerated.

In eastern Turkey sex before marriage is completely taboo.

Relationship duress is not difficult to understand if you understand the reasons why it's in place.

The Sex 2.0 society, which we all grew up in, is essentially a cult. It's a cult because of the two-planes-of-sexuality schism, along with the requisite bullying and cajoling of people into accepting only one of them.

We don't think of Sex 2.0 society as a cult because it's all pervasive, but the definition of *cult* is illuminating:

**cult** - *noun*

> A group of people that follow unnatural practices which are socially enforced

As human sexual nature is marginalised in Sex 2.0 society and people follow "normal" (in other words unnatural) practices the cultish nature of Sex 2.0 society starts to become clear.

As for it being "socially enforced", what is RD? RD *is* social enforcement. Sex 2.0 society is an exact dictionary definition of a cult; a group of people that follow unnatural practices which are socially enforced.

Sex 2.0 RD is basically society strapping blinkers on people and shoving them down a narrow corridor. If you blindly stumble down this corridor, it goes like this:

Dating -> boyfriend/girlfriend -> marriage

(Skip the first two parts if you live in a culture of arranged marriages)

I am not suggesting that dating is bad, nor I am suggesting that bf/gf or marital relationships are bad. None of these are bad if they are what you truly have chosen, rather than choosing them for reasons of RD.

Any relationship that's loving and pair-bonded, in which both parties find mutual reward, is a true and legitimate relationship regardless of whether it is fenced or unfenced.

However, relationship duress in our Sex 2.0 world is ratcheted up to the point where the "choice" of a fenced relationship is not usually a choice at all, but an obligation.

Since fenced is a societal obligation, then Sex 2.0 is by definition dogmatic. It involves living your life by other people's values and beliefs, whether or not you freely agree with them.

Society says that if you don't go along with this obligation, you are up to no good.

Why would society be so terribly threatened by those who choose unfenced from the very beginning of the relationship? The answer is that people have to stay convinced that they've made the right choice when they decided that the normal plane is the correct plane.

People will project their fears onto you and insist that their maps and their choices are correct.

They will probably make a basic error like insisting that their map *is* the territory, or that the map was drawn by an invisible sky god and so is not to be questioned.

They will not realise something very important, which is that the most valid choices in life are the ones you truly choose. The less valid are choices made by default because you don't think you have a choice. The least valid choices of all are the ones made under duress.

When it comes to the choice of fenced or unfenced, there is no "right" choice; there is only the choice that is right for you.

# 19 – Jealousy and Possessiveness

The normal sexual plane—along with the relationship duress necessary for enforcing it in the new sexual marketplace--was not the only huge change at the dawn of Sex 2.0.

As a terrible side-effect of the Sex 2.0 revolution, a hideous, ugly, twin-headed monster was spat out into this world for the first time.

And although this monster was born many thousands of years ago, it is not only still alive today—it's actually stronger today than ever. It wreaks havoc and causes more emotional pain and misery in human relationships than anything else.

The twin-headed monster is jealousy and possessiveness.

Globally, this monster causes multiple violent human deaths every single day of the year, as well as many, many non-fatal beatings, stabbings, shootings, acid attacks and all kinds of other insanity.

Today this monster is so powerful and prevalent that many people mistakenly believe that its presence is unavoidable and that they have to live with it, and of course this belief is enforced by relationships duress.

All over the world, mothers tell their teenage sons and daughters who come home upset after their first serious argument with their first serious gf or bf, "Honey, you're not the first couple in the world to have a fight. It'll be ok. It'll be all right. Couples fight. That's just what they do."

The arguments are almost always over some jealous/possessive bullshit.

I'm sure mothers feel they're being helpful and loving by comforting offspring that way, never realising that they're perpetuating the most dangerous possible error on their vulnerable teenagers' "How Sexual Relationships are Supposed to Work" map.

The dangerous error is the idea that human sexual relationships are *supposed* to be difficult and you just have to accept it.

If you still are carrying that error on your map, then erase it now! It's the biggest and worst error you can possibly have on your map.

Human sexual relationships are *not* supposed to be difficult. They are supposed to be every bit as self-sustaining and effortless as any loving friendship.

Later on in the book you will see how, but first we need to take a look at the role the twin-headed monster plays in fenced relationships.

## The Twin-Headed Monster Sequence

The very concept itself of sexual ownership (being fenced) actively promotes jealousy and possessiveness, and it's the same twin-headed monster that destroys all fenced relationships. Ok, not *all* of them, but easily more than 50%.

Jealousy and possessiveness are the primary killers of fenced relationships.

Fenced relationships are not only founded on the concept of sexual ownership, but also are completely permeated by it, and they are extremely predictable.

The simple five-step sequence goes like this:

**Stage 1 – boy meets girl**

**Stage 2 – boy and girl find that they have a very cool connection together**

**Stage 3 – connection becomes sexual and they start a sexual relationship**

At this stage—step three—everything's great. In fact, everything's better than great--it's perfect! This is the romantic infatuation stage.

Women are especially happy, because all their emotions are telling them that not only are they following the fairy-princess-get-married-and-live-happily-ever-after script, but they are following it successfully! It's actually working! This is what a real relationship is supposed to be like!

Guys at this stage are head over heels in love, totally infatuated, and giddy. All is well with the world.

If both parties are infatuated, then at this point both will think that maybe, just maybe, they have found "the one."

Both men and women during this stage exhibit an exceptionally high level of relationship duress and will happily lecture friends about how this is the way all true relationships are meant to be, that this is the perfect recipe for true happiness. They will dismiss anything that might even hint otherwise (including this book).

So everything is great and perfect until.....the jealous possessive bullshit kicks in.

When that happens, the relationship enters…

**Step 4 – the spin cycle**

The spin cycle stage goes around and around like a tumble dyer or washing machine, like this:

Everything is great for a while -> argue about jealous/possessive bullshit -> make up (often involving make-up sex) -> everything is great for a while *until* the next time you argue about jealous/possessive bullshit (rinse and repeat).

The problem in arguing with the person you're in a relationship with is that you poison the connection between you.

The problem with the make-up sex is that it's sometimes so intense and great that it feels like you've removed the poison from the connection.

You haven't.

This is a temporary delusion brought on by the cocktail of hormones running through your veins which acts like a painkiller and, like all painkillers, it inevitably wears off.

You have not removed the poison from the connection or solved the problem because the root cause of the problem – sexual ownership – is still built into the very foundation of the relationship.

And no--it does not matter how long you lie in each other's arms in post-coital make-up sex bliss, staring deeply into each other's eyes saying "you know Baby I hate arguing with you," and both pledging with sincere determination never ever to argue again.

It does not matter because nothing has changed. Sexual ownership will *still* promote jealousy and possessiveness, so the next argument is guaranteed; it's just a question of time.

And so the relationship goes on for months and years, spinning around the stage-four spin cycle.

Towards the end of the spin cycle, makeup sex eventually becomes just a painkiller that brings only temporary relief between ever-more-frequent arguments.

Each argument poisons the connection more and more, until eventually the connection becomes so toxic that it has to be severed, and you reach....

## Stage 5 – the Breakup

It does not matter if you or your partner cuts the connection, or if the breakup is mutual—the end result is exactly the same.

The result is that the person you once had a really cool connection with is now no longer in your life.

You know what? That sucks.

If you are reading this and have experienced a significant number of fenced relationships, then you almost certainly will recognise this five-step sequence.

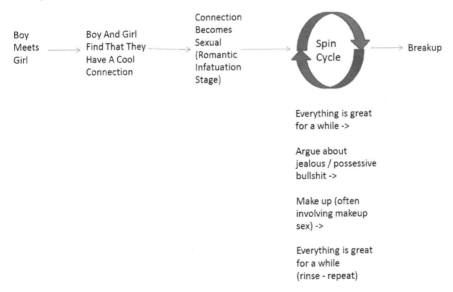

When you're conscious of this sequence and have been through it enough times to recognise it clearly, you come to a very simple conclusion:

Having jealousy and possessiveness in your life means *you always suffer.*

Read that last sentence again.

If you find that yourself following this five-step sequence over and over again in your sexual relationships, then consider getting that sentence tattooed on the inside of your eyelids so that you'll never forget it.

When you have jealousy and possessiveness in your life, *you always suffer.*

Even if you are not jealous or possessive, it doesn't matter, because if your partner *is* jealous or possessive you will still suffer because they will argue with you about it.

If you understand that when you have jealousy and possessiveness in your life you always suffer, you can ask yourself a very simple question that leads to a simple choice:

Would you like to suffer or would you like to not suffer?

Choose.

Would you like to suffer in this way, or would you like to not suffer?

Choose now.

If you've chosen not to suffer, then you've made a wise choice.

In the Sex 3.0 section of the book I will tell you how not to suffer in this way. First, however, we need to look at a few more things about the Sex 2.0 marketplace, and how to deal with them.

# 20 – The Corruption of Love

If you've been wondering why a book about relationships has not been talking about love very much, there's a good reason.

Love--across Sex 1.0, Sex 2.0 and Sex 3.0--has never changed, not one bit. What I mean by that is that there are no differences in love itself that are equivalent to each stage of human history.

Love is insanely simple. If you love someone, you just want them to be happy--that's it.

We understand this intuitively because we all have friends and family members that we love. How do you feel for the people you love, and what do you want from them or for them?

You just want them to be happy. You want them to be well and to have a good life--the best life possible. You want them to have good health and to be safe from harm, and you feel these things as a very deep emotional need.

If you love somebody in a sexual relationship, the reason you're with them is not because you're afraid of being unable to find anyone else, nor because you want or need something from them, be it security, sexual exclusivity, compliance, money or anything else.

Love is also not romantic infatuation. During the early infatuation period, it is not uncommon for your body to be flooded with chemicals like phenylethylamine, dopamine and other endorphins similar to opiates. You are literally on drugs.

Unfortunately these aren't the kind of drugs that will make you wail on the guitar like Hendrix--just the kind that make everything seem positive, put a big dopey smile on your face and give you a sense of wellbeing.

What I call "Love Junkie Syndrome" is the way a person in this phase often neglects their friends, takes the side of their lover in any dispute whether or not their lover is right, and lashes out at anything they feel threatens their "stash" of love-junkie endorphins.

Many people refer to the romantic infatuation phase as "being in love" but unlike love, romantic infatuation is ephemeral. Its nature is transitory and short-lived.

Love is what is left when the endorphins wear off.

Many people think that a little jealousy is good in a relationship because it shows that your partner cares. I disagree. Jealousy is a negative emotion--a feeling of terrible and sometimes crushing insecurity.

If you enjoy observing that feeling in your partner because it eases your own insecurity as to whether they care about you or not, then essentially you are enjoying the suffering of someone you claim to love.

This is a win/lose situation, in which your feeling good depends on your partner feeling bad, or vice versa.

This is the opposite of love; it's a corruption of love.

*"Jealousy is a disease, love is a healthy condition. The immature mind often mistakes one for the other, or assumes that the greater the love, the greater the jealousy - in fact they*

*are almost incompatible; one emotion hardly leaves room for the other." - Robert Heinlein*

Love is nothing more or less than the deep emotional need for the happiness and wellbeing of another--a feeling so deep that it's integral to your own happiness. To see them happy makes you happy.

Love is certainly not the desire to own someone. Ownership is also a corruption of love.

We have become, during the 2.0 era, extremely skilled at rationalising away the poisonous consequences of Sex 2.0. We do this to justify to ourselves and to each other our continued allegiance to the normal, unnatural love paradigm.

Commitment = sexual ownership? No it doesn't. Commitment to someone means returning when you have a choice not to.

Wouldn't it be better to know that your partner is with you because he or she wants to be and not because they are fulfilling a societal obligation or are legally handcuffed to you in marriage?

We argue because we love each other so much? No. Anger and insecurity are about as far away from love as you can get. Love is simply a deep emotional concern for the wellbeing of another.

Love hurts? No it doesn't. Love feels great whether you are on the receiving end of it or are experiencing it yourself.

You always hurt the ones you love most? This is a very silly idea. Pain is the last thing you want for someone you love. See if the following sentences make any sense to you:

> • She's such a loving person; she's always so jealous and insecure.

> • He's such a loving person; he's always hitting her and telling her what to do.

These beliefs are confused and wrong.

Sex 2.0 corrupts love, so much so that many adults and even famous philosophers struggle with it. So, let's leave the last word in this chapter for someone too young to have been corrupted on the subject of love.

*"Love is when my mommy makes coffee for my daddy and she takes a sip before giving it to him, to make sure the taste is OK." - Danny, age 7*

Yes, that's it--that's real love right there.

# 21 – Monogamy Is a Sexual Perversion

Since there are only two types of sexual relationship--fenced and unfenced--there are only two possible ways in which they can become false-fenced. Let's look into both.

First we'll look at the far more popular one, which is so wonderfully popular that practically the entire world does it.

### False Fencing the Normal Plane

Two major forces--push and pull--are at work in the Sex 2.0 world.

People are pushed by relationship duress into fenced relationships, and pulled by the gravitational draw of human nature, over a period of time, towards unfenced.

As a result, the majority of relationships that begin as fenced relationships inevitably are dragged into a false-fenced state. That is to say, one or both parties hop over the fence while the other one is not looking.

The sequence goes like this:

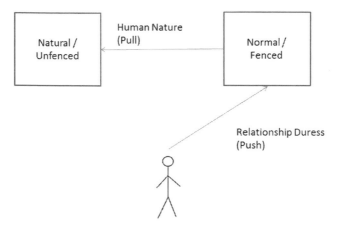

Secretly hopping over the fence turns a fenced relationship into a false-fenced relationship, which is a ticking time bomb.

If you're reading this and you currently have a false-fenced relationship and are feeling smug because you haven't been found out yet, be forewarned. All you've done is strapped sticks of dynamite to the four pillars, closed your eyes and spun the timer on the detonator. You don't know *when* you're going to get found out, but when the detonator goes the pillars will collapse.

I'm referring of course to the four pillars of pure form relationships:

**Communication** – You are not communicating to your partner your true desires or needs.

**Honesty** – Not only are you lying, you are cheating and deceiving.

**Trust** – You are showing that you cannot be trusted.

**Respect** – Roping in another person's sexuality on condition that you do the same and then going back on the deal behind their back is one of the most disrespectful things you can possibly do to another person.

Why would you do all of this to somebody you love?

I am not saying this to be judgemental. In the first half of my adult sex life I attempted fenced relationships because, like many people, I thought that was what you were "supposed to do." I falsely believed that I didn't really have a choice and that's what you had to do if you wanted a long term sexual relationship. That's exactly what society was telling me.

The result was false-fenced relationships, and based on research and a lifetime of observation, I am not alone in this regard.

If you take the average human lifespan to be approximately 78 years, that means you have about 60 years of adulthood. Comprehensive surveys have shown that during a 30-year sexual relationship, four fifths of women and two thirds of men admit to being unfaithful--leaving only 13 percent of relationships that remain truly fenced for a 30-year period.[xxiii]

When you factor in the exceptionally high number of relationships that don't even last that long due to infidelity, and all of the relationships where partners actually embark on an affair as a way of getting out of a relationship, the percentage of false-fenced relationships in the normal plane is clearly in the high 90s.

Lifetime monogamy--"normalised" only very recently in human history--never has been natural to human beings, is not natural now, and is not going to become natural in the millennia to come.

It is patently obvious from objective consideration that humankind is not well served by the pretence that lifetime monogamy is natural.

Pretending that lifetime monogamy is natural is self-deception, pure and simple. It is a fraud perpetrated on the self, and a denial of the very core of human nature.

Of course, people can always talk about the exceptions. We all know couples who have been happily married for 50-odd years. We can point to them and say, "Well what about these guys? *They* made it work!"

Well, yes they did. And we can equally say when there's a train wreck that there are usually survivors who walk away from the wreckage miraculously without a scratch.

But we don't stand at the wreck site ignoring all the wounded and all the people in horrible pain, while pointing to miraculous survivors and saying, "Hey, look at these guys--not a scratch on them! That means a train wreck isn't a bad thing!"

To stretch this metaphor a little further, we can view the relationship duress you live under as the stationmaster standing on the platform shouting "All aboard now! Everyone get on the Sex 2.0 train wreck" as it leaves the platform and heads along its inevitable collision course.

Furthermore, you have no way of knowing for sure if a couple with the longstanding marriage referred to above has a relationship that is fenced or false-fenced.

This is exactly the kind of truth that parents are loath to tell children. I've heard many stories during my research of people who are shocked to discover that their still happily-married parents have a false-fenced relationship in which one or both has been unfaithful at some point.

## *False Fencing the Natural Plane*

The other type of false-fenced relationship is one in which you both verbally agree to an unfenced relationship but still do the "jealousy/possessiveness" thing.

If you are being jealous and/or possessive in an unfenced relationship, or if your partner is and you tolerate it, then you are not in an unfenced relationship--you are in a fenced relationship.

That relationship is also false-fenced, except that it went like this:

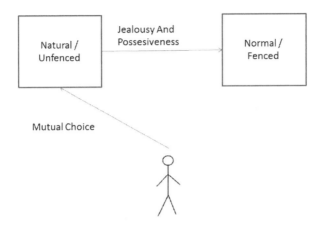

You have apparently agreed on unfenced, but emotionally you are fenced.

This does not work either, for two reasons. First:

**Jealousy and possessiveness have absolutely no place in unfenced relationships.**

If someone wants a relationship based on sexual ownership, including all the jealous and possessive bullshit that typically accompanies it, then that's their choice. But they need to choose the normal plane, and they need to choose to be fenced.

That's what fenced relationships are designed for, and that's what you should choose if you want it.

Second:

**Fenced and unfenced are like oil and water; they don't mix.**

Consciously choose one sexual plane or the other. Whatever you do, don't mix the two.

## The Sex 2.0 Norm

I did not write a chapter title like "Monogamy Is a Sexual Perversion" to be controversial. Stating what is obvious is not usually considered controversial.

Not only is it obvious that enforced monogamy is a deviation from nature, but another thing is very obvious as well:

In the Sex 2.0 marketplace, cheating is the norm. Why? We'll look at that in the next few chapters.

# 22 – The Pacman, the Slut and the Whore

Also introduced at the start of the Sex 2.0 marketplace were sluts and whores.

Whilst both "slut" and "whore" are fairly meaningless, shaming words to me, it's worth taking a look at why society started using them, and why there are no equivalent insults for men.

## The PACman

The root cause of both words is "PACmen."

I don't mean the cute video game character, I mean the concern about paternity that the fenced relationship agenda is designed to alleviate. We addressed in previous chapters that the fenced agenda is universal, and not because fenced relationships are so perfect or are the correct way to go.

In the "Birth of Sex 2.0" chapter we covered the fact that because females are the ones who actually give birth, they do not have the same concern. Paternity concern (or PAC for short) is universal, and the world is filled with PACmen.

Young boys are conditioned to grow into PACmen at an insanely young age. Boys who have not even gone through puberty yet and who have a girlfriend at school that they maybe hold hands with or kiss are conditioned to be outraged and repulsed by girls who have kissed or held hands with "too many" boys.

"Too many" often means just *two*--as opposed to only one boy. Even though the boy is physically not mature enough to have any justifiable paternity concern, and cannot even have sex yet, the stage is set.

PACmen spread as the agricultural revolution spread. That started roughly 8,000 years BC, and gradually went global, along with the concept of property.

Although no countries formally existed in 8,000 BC (because there can be no countries without the concept of property, only tribes), agriculture developed in parts of North Africa and the Middle East and Asia, and spread from there.[xxiv]

It arrived in other countries much later. In the USA, for example, agriculture arrived only as recently as several *hundred* years ago when the Europeans brought it and the concept of property with them.

Before that the Native Americans were hunter gatherers. They did grow certain staple items but the crucial point is that they didn't depend on those for their survival. They depended on hunting and gathering.

Almost all societies in the world currently are Sex 2.0 societies, because of the global spread of PACmen and the concept of property.

## The Slut

If you are a woman who has sex with a guy *without any thought of establishing a fenced relationship with him*, but simply for your own reasons – because you think the guy is attractive, or you think you'd find the sex satisfying, or you haven't had sex for a while, or for any reason related to satisfying your needs without thought of a fenced relationship with him--then society has a delightful word reserved for you: *slut.*

This word is used not just by men but by women too.

Why do women call women sluts? Well, first we need to understand that the word has two different meanings, depending on whether a man or a woman is using it. Both men and women wield the word as a shaming weapon, but differently.

When a man calls a woman a slut, even if he isn't having sex with her, he's saying she is either:

> A. Having more sex than he approves of, which triggers his PAC and wakes up the twin-headed monster, or

> B. She's advertising her sexuality in a way that triggers his PAC and wakes up the twin-headed monster

The female response is simply to be more covert about sexuality or sexual dalliances, or else to not care and just ignore him if she doesn't regard him as important.

When a woman calls a woman a slut, on the other hand, it means something different …

Imagine you have sunk your entire life saving into, let's say, opening a DVD store to sell all the latest movies. You proudly open your store, and then on the first day of business you see someone setting up a temporary stall right outside the front of it, with pirate copies of the very same movies. Not only that, but they're not even selling them—they're giving them away for free! Outrage!

When a woman calls a woman a slut, she's accusing her of breaking the Sex 2.0 deal—the unwritten rule that says that all women have to sell their sexuality in exchange for security.

When a woman calls another woman a slut she's saying "You're giving away for free something that I believe I need to sell in order to survive!"

She's saying, "This can't be allowed! You must be shamed into not behaving in this way! We all have to club together as sisters to shame you, and reinforce a society in which such behaviour cheapens your sexual marketplace value so greatly that no man will want to buy your sexuality (marry you) because it's so worthless!"

In other words, when women call another woman a slut they are accusing her of being a traitor to her own gender.

Women essentially police other women by shaming each other in this manner, because they believe they need to do so to ensure that the Sex 2.0 deal stays in place and remains viable. All women who don't follow the agenda are breaking "union rules."

Of course in saying that, I am presuming that the woman being labelled a slut is not doing so because she is upset over the sexual competition for a man she is interested in.

Sexual competition is quite a different case, and in my country (England) women use a different but equally unpleasant word for each other when they experience sexual competition. Here it's "slag," and I believe the word "tramp" is the American equivalent.

## The Whore

The word "slut" is suitably shaming for women who commit the terrible offence of breaking the Sex 2.0 deal (i.e. not selling their sexuality *at all*), but society needs another shaming word for women who *do* sell their sexuality.

These women don't sell sex exclusively to one guy in exchange for security, but rather for cold hard cash. The word for that of course is "whore."

Society says that whores must be shamed too. Why? Not only do whores fall outside of the Sex 2.0 deal, but they offer men a way of following their genetic imperative without having to satisfy a woman's genetic imperative in return. Whores offer men a "get out" clause from the Sex 2.0 deal!

Horror of horrors! Society reserves a special level of vitriol for these women. Why?

Well, like sluts, whores offer men what they want–sex–without making them provide security in return. But unlike sluts, whores are attempting to attain their *own financial security* without selling their sexuality exclusively for life to one man. This is a far greater threat to the Sex 2.0 deal.

In return their social status is relegated to the very bottom rung of society.

Whores hate sluts too, because sluts give away something that they are trying to sell or at least rent, which of course is pussy.

The word "harlot" is often confused with whore because the only difference between them is the type and method of payment.

A harlot is a woman who has sex with a man because she expects something (other than sex or cash) in return, and will cease offering sex to him should it not be forthcoming.

It doesn't matter whether it's free drinks, meals and movies, increased access to influential people (celebrities, rock stars etc.), a role in a film, a shot at musical stardom, or the promise of a free holiday.

If there's any direct connection in her head between "putting out" and what she gets in return, and if she stops putting out when she stops bringing in, then she's a harlot.

Interestingly, the word "harlot," first recorded in the English language in the 13th century, initially referred to a *man*.

Back then a harlot was the kind of man who was a beggar or vagabond--a man who seeks not mutual reward in his relationships with others, but who takes value and offers no reward in return.

In the 14th century the word first appeared as a derogatory term for a woman, and by the end of the 17th century it was no longer used to refer to men at all. It was co-opted to be a weapon in society's fight against anything other than the status quo of fenced relationships.[xxv]

Slut also originated in the English language (in the 15th century) to mean something else. Slut at first meant slovenly, untidy, unclean or careless, but it too was co-opted in service of the on-going Sex 2.0 agenda.[xxvi]

## The Cruel Choice

So this is the cruel choice that society presents to women: sell your sexuality in exchange for security and legally handcuff yourself to a man and become his wife (or at least be seen to be trying to do so by being his girlfriend)--and if you don't, then you are a slut, whore, harlot or a dyke.

Charming!

Of course the entire slut/whore paradigm is nothing more than relationship duress (RD), pure and simple.

In a Sex 2.0 world, the only refuge for women from this kind of RD is to adopt the in-between role of girlfriend with a sole boyfriend in a fenced relationship. That's the only get-out-of-jail-free card that liberates you from this kind of relationship duress.

This way, at least in most modern cultures, women can avoid being shamed and insulted. Unsurprisingly, many opt for an entire lifetime of serial monogamy as a result.

They go from boyfriend to boyfriend and tolerate the "when are you getting married?" kind of RD that they face because it is mild by comparison.

Problem solved? Well, in a word: no.

Sex 2.0 society has come up with a whole lot of social imperatives (the normal plane) that are in direct conflict with the genetic imperatives of human beings (the natural plane).

Human beings are not monogamous by nature--neither men nor women. Therefore society forces both sexes into duplicity—one that is relatively easy to maintain in the early infatuation stage of a relationship, but not for life. That duplicity inevitably resolves itself over a period of time by the false fencing of the normal plane.

Since the social imperatives do not respect the fact that sex is a basic human need; do not respect human nature; and do not respect the genetic imperatives, they are themselves unnatural and against nature.

Who came up with them?

## The Cruel Choice Committee

Picture a committee meeting of women, called together thousands and thousands of years ago.

**Speaker**:  Thank you all for coming, Ladies. This meeting has been called into order to decide what we should all do about sex.

**Woman 1**: Sex?

**Speaker**: Yes, sex. How it should be treated?

**Woman 1**: Well isn't sex just a basic human need like eating, drinking and sleeping. Shouldn't we just treat it like any other basic human need?

**Woman 2**: Interesting concept. So you are saying that we should have sex with just anyone?

**Woman 1**: No, I am not saying that at all. I am saying that we women should have sex with whomever *we choose* and for any reason that *we choose*.

**Woman 3**: Interesting, but I have a better idea. How about we do exactly as you suggest and have sex with whomever we choose, for any reason that we choose—and then society, both men and women, roundly condemns us and insults us and makes us feel cheap and worthless?

**Women 4,5,6,7 and 8**: Yay! That sounds great!

**Woman 4**: Oh, I like that idea. Let's do that. If we indulge in this basic human need everybody will make us feel cheap and worthless!

**Woman 5**: I *love* the idea that everyone insults us!

**Woman 3**: What woman wouldn't love that?!

**Woman 5**: Ooooooh!! Ohhhhh!! I just thought of a way to improve it.

**Woman 4**: How?

**Woman 5**: How about if we allow women to have sex without being insulted *only* if they engage exclusively in sexual relationships based on the concept of sexual ownership and all of the jealousy and possessiveness that comes with it?

**Woman 1**: Wait, why would we do that?

**Woman 5**: So we can sell our sexuality in exchange for security, of course!

**Woman 1**: What if we don't need to? I mean what if we have our own career, home, money and can provide our own security?

*awkward pause*

*shuffling of papers*

**Speaker**: that doesn't matter—the same rules apply. (Bangs gavel on table)

**All**: Yaaayy!

**Woman 4**: Oh, I *love* jealous possessive bullshit!

**Speaker**: Agreed! So from now on everybody has to insult and degrade us and make us feel cheap and worthless whenever we engage in this basic human need---*unless* we sell our sexuality in exchange for security in relationships based on sexual ownership, jealousy and possessiveness!

**Woman 5**: Awesome! Just one thing. How are we going to convince the guys to go along with this agenda?

**Speaker**: Simple. We just tell them that we won't fuck them unless they do.

**All**: Yaaayy!

But of course that's not what happened…..

Even though women's needs for security and protection in modern western society used to be much greater (before reliable contraceptives and female careers existed), it is *men* who came up with these social imperatives to deal with their PAC.

Getting women to buy into Sex 2.0 and play a leading role in repressing the sexuality of their own gender is probably the single biggest con job pulled over on them since the beginning of time.

If you are a woman and you ever call another woman a slut or whore (unless it's meant as a joke or a playful tease), then you're participating in the repression.

The cruel choice committee put women in an impossible position, in which they are judged by both men and women their entire lives.

Sex is a basic human need and nothing more than that. It is a need for which nobody should be judged.

# 23 – How Did We Get Into This Mess?

If you're thinking that we already covered this question in the previous chapters, what we covered really was the "why" of the matter. The "how" of it is also worth looking at.

And this might help to clarify something else. It may have sounded in the last chapter as if I blamed men for the current situation, but that would be overly simplistic.

The cruel choice committee may have been mostly men, but the current situation arose as the result of "groupthink." It resulted from both men and women trying to wrestle with PAC and the invention of property in a mostly patriarchal era.

The interesting study of groupthink in human behavioural psychology illuminates the process of hive-mind decision-making within tightly-knit social groups.

The Asch conformity experiments I mentioned in an earlier chapter is probably the most famous test of conformity in human beings, but they were conducted with subjects who were strangers—i.e. not in any kind of tightly-knit social group. The field of groupthink is quite different but no less fascinating.

Much of the initial work in this field was done by Irving Janis, a research psychologist from Yale University who defined

Groupthink as "a mode of thinking that people engage in when they are deeply involved in a cohesive in-group, when the members' strivings for unanimity override their motivation to realistically appraise alternative courses of action." [xxvii]

In other words, the desire for cohesive harmony of the group overrides realistic evaluation of more highly-functioning alternatives, and prevents critical evaluation of flaws of the decisions of the group for fear of disrupting group cohesion.

Another psychologist (T Hart) defined it as "collective optimism and collective avoidance."

Although the initial fieldwork was done by Janis some time later, I believe the term groupthink was coined by American journalist William H. Whyte in 1952. Whyte said, "What we are talking about is a rationalised conformity--an open, articulate philosophy which holds that group values are not only expedient but right and good as well."

So many errors on people's relationship maps result from the replacement of independent critical thinking with groupthink.

Groupthink compounds the problems by groupthink-based prevention of contradictory or counter-doctrinal views (e.g. the view that enforced monogamy might not be such a good thing after all).

Groupthink keeps alternate ideas from being expressed, considered and reasonably evaluated. The status quo is enforced with relationship duress, which causes dissenting voices to be stamped out and dissenting ideas to be labelled illegitimate.

One of the common characteristics of groupthink is the group's belief in the *morality* of the group and the *immorality* of those outside the group.

Another common sign of groupthink is the illusion of the invulnerability of the model of thought that the group has agreed on.

Growing up in a Sex 2.0 world, do you see those signs around you when it comes to sexual relationships?

If you've ever attended a wedding ceremony and heard a vicar or priest wax lyrical about morals and the solidity of the institution of marriage, then you've experienced groupthink. Clergy are not the only ones who do it--society as a whole does it—but clergy are the ones who make it their job.

In addition to belief in inherent morality and the illusion of invulnerability, Janis identified six more symptoms of groupthink:

> 1 --Collective rationalization. Members discount warnings and do not reconsider their assumptions.
>
> 2 - Stereotyped views of out-groups. Negative views of the "enemy" make effective responses to conflict seem unnecessary.
>
> 3 - Direct pressure on dissenters. Members are under pressure not to express arguments against any of the group's views.
>
> 4 - Self-censorship. Doubts and deviations from the perceived group consensus are not expressed.
>
> 5 - Illusion of unanimity. The majority view and judgments are assumed to be unanimous.
>
> 6 - Self-appointed "mind guards." Members protect the group and the leader from information that is problematic or contradictory to the group's cohesiveness, view, and/or decisions.

So, to answer the question of how we got into this mess:

In a Sex 2.0 world, we are all victims of groupthink when it comes to how sexual relationships are supposed to work.

Don't want to be a victim any more? Well, the only one who can change that is you.

Between now and the end of the book, you will see how you can do just that.

# 24 – Revenge of the Nerds

As mentioned in the chapter on the Sex 2.0 genetic imperative, the female genetic imperative changed when we moved from Sex 1.0 to Sex 2.0. It changed from only one primary imperative:

> 1 - Seek high quality alpha male DNA and physical protection and security for both self and child (socio)

...to both a primary imperative (socio) and a secondary imperative (economic):

> 1 - Seek high quality alpha male DNA and physical protection and security for both self and child (socio)

> 2 - Seek a partner who can provide financial security for self and children. Prevent other women from diluting such an arrangement (economic)

(The second imperative, as we've seen, reflects the fact that property/money became an important survival resource thousands of years ago.)

In modern western countries today, where women have access to social mobility, careers and their own money, they may or may not need to seek a partner for financial security. Even if they don't, the second imperative still has a number of interesting effects on modern society and the Sex 2.0 marketplace, like:

## The Spectrum Correction

The arrival of the second female genetic imperative was a good thing for beta males. The nerds were about to get their revenge.

As you may recall, the spectrum dilemma in a Sex 1.0 world meant that males polarised at either ends of the spectrum-- alpha and beta.

Alphas got all the female attention and betas lived a mostly sexless existence and were, by and large, genetically weeded out of existence.

In a Sex 2.0 world however, a beta can be rich, and even though he can't satisfy the first imperative, he can now satisfy the second.

In the Sex 1.0 world the beta was a peripheral figure whereas in the Sex 2.0 marketplace a beta clearly has an important role to play.

In fact, although he cannot satisfy a woman's primary need for an alpha male, a beta can satisfy some parts of the primary imperative, since that includes the need for security and protection which can now be purchased.

The modern-day provision of security and protection has changed from fighting off predatory animals and violent men. Now, predatory animals are taken care of by the authorities, and violent men get sent to prison.

Modern-day security and protection mainly means a warm home, so the radical polarisation of the male spectrum that existed in the Sex 1.0 world has been corrected. Now there's a sprinkling of men all along the alpha-beta spectrum.

In current society, some men are very alpha (although a lot of those might be locked up in prisons), and some are very beta (although a lot of those might be locked up in their mom's basement playing World of Warcraft), but mostly there is a large sprinkling of men along the spectrum that have some alpha traits and some beta traits.

## The Most Important Imperative

Bearing in mind that the sole male imperative has always been, and remains, to have sex with lots of fertile women, you might be wondering why men didn't develop a second imperative at the same time women did.

Since property and money became important survival resources--important enough for women to develop a second imperative—then why didn't men?

Well, because we did not need to.

Simply being an alpha continued to work very well if you wanted to get laid and still does today.

Lots of guys mistakenly believe that they need money and "bling" to get female attention. In fact, an entire industry is funded and fuelled by these guys--it's called the nightclub industry.

These are the guys deluded into thinking that impressing girls with "bling" and overpriced bottle service is the way to go, and that a good pick-up line is "Hey baby your eyes are the same colour as my Porsche." They think there's something wrong with women who roll their eyes in response, and then tell themselves "She's probably a lesbian" as they insist that their map is correct and reality is wrong.

Don't be that guy. If you are that guy, erase that part of your map. Do it now.

If you think you need signs of wealth to get chicks, then understand that this is a false idea put forward by advertisers to sell you flashy stuff you don't even need. Of course governments love this because it helps keep you slaving away in your cubicle and keeps the taxes rolling in.

So why does being an alpha still work just fine? Because women do not need to have the same man satisfy both biological imperatives--and they often don't.

Women can regard one guy as good "marriage material," (in other words a good provider), and another guy as a good fuck, just because he's a fuckable guy (i.e. dominant, confident, socially proofed, or just because other women want him).

Of women's two imperatives, clearly the primary imperative is the most important in modern society.

## A General Election in a Dictatorship

One of the things that have often puzzled archaeologists is the odd discovery that human skeletons in cultures that went through the agricultural revolution show clear signs of shrinking in the years following the transition. The shrinking was so great that only today have human beings recovered the physical size we had back when we were hunter-gathers.

The shrinkage seems odd, considering that the agricultural revolution was about the invention of a superior, less dangerous and less exhausting way to feed ourselves.

Many theorists have concluded that the culprit is the change from a hunter-gatherer type of diet to the diet of a farmer.

I have another theory, which is that average physical size decreased due to betas' success at producing offspring in large numbers for the first time.

Beta males at the time would have been generally physically smaller and less strong than alphas, and in a Sex 1.0 world they would not really have had a chance sexually. In a post-agricultural society, on the other hand, they not only get a chance sexually--they also get to hold a general election in a genetic dictatorship.

What I mean is that, for practically all of human history, sexual relationships were unfenced--meaning that there was no enforced monogamy. Sperm competition and the survival of the fittest was the order of the day in the genetic pool.

It was not really possible to pass down weak genetic features like low fertility and low sperm count.

Enter fenced relationships and enforced monogamy, and for the first time in human history, weak genetic features like low fertility and low sperm count can now be passed down.

In a dictatorship it doesn't matter how few people turn up to vote, the same guy is always going to win.

## Two Ways Men and Women Drive Each Other Crazy

As a result of the introduction of the secondary female imperative into the Sex 2.0 marketplace, men and women developed two ways in which they would drive each other crazy. I don't mean crazy in a good way--I mean it in a really bad way.

But since we developed one each, let's call it evens.

The next two chapters look at each of them in turn.

# 25 – Why Women Nag Men

Why do women henpeck men, and why is there no male equivalent?

The male equivalent of a hen is a rooster, but men don't rooster-peck women.

Think about this for a minute before you read further, and see what theory you can come up with.

There must be a reason, and no--the answer is not that women really enjoy complaining, because they really don't. Trust me; a lifetime of experience might tell you otherwise, but they really don't.

I have also heard people theorise that it's just in women's nature to nag. I disagree with that too, as well as with the popular theory that women nag because they are dominant and domineering (bullies).

Men being nagged don't understand why it's happening, and say that they don't "get" women. They often complain that it starts the moment they get inside the front door: "What time do you call this?" "Why didn't you take the rubbish out?" "When are you going to mow the damn lawn?"

And they don't understand why things that in the beginning of the relationship she found cute, she now finds so annoying. They don't understand why she constantly flies off the handle, so they tell themselves that she's "just plain crazy" and convince themselves they're being nagged for "no apparent reason."

That's a mapping error right there, and a really big one. There *is* a reason, but the woman is never going to tell you what it is. The reason she won't tell you what it is, is that she doesn't know herself.

I've never met a woman who can give a good answer to the question of why women henpeck men but men don't rooster-peck women.

When a woman is nagging her man and you stop and ask her why, she won't tell you. She'll simply give you a list of things she's dissatisfied with, without telling the real root cause of the dissatisfaction.

They might say it's a result of "always having to do every damn thing," or it's "not being listened to," or it's due to the immaturity of their partner. They aren't lying when they say that because they honestly believe it's the case.

All they really know is that they're feeling unhappy.

Women's not knowing the real root cause is obviously a *huge* problem, because guys make the mistake of listening to the answers they get and then attempting to problem-solve in a logical, rational way based on this bad information.

Sometimes guys don't even get bad information; they are just faced with an upset woman who says, "Well, if you don't know why I'm upset then I'm not going to tell you!" She says this because she doesn't know the answer herself. She wants the guy to work out the answer and solve the problem.

Don't worry—you're going to find out the answer in this chapter.

You have to pity the poor guys. We've all witnessed the grocery store scene and felt a withering sense of pity for how he's getting relentlessly henpecked and hammered into submission. To feel badly for him is the only really human response.

What are guys left with? All they can do is use avoidance tactics like spending time in the pub with their male buddies, zoning out and not listening, and just occasionally reply with an "ok" or the odd "uh huh" as they bury their head deeper and deeper in the newspaper.

Of course this doesn't solve the problem either and will only increase the distance between the couple and further heighten resentment.

The guy's map tells him, quite incorrectly, that she's going to nag no matter what and that nagging is just one of the prices you pay for being in a long term relationship.

This is a major mapping error. If you are a guy and you have that mapping error and you do break up with your girl because you can't take the nagging any more then, guess what?

Your next girl is going to nag at you too.

I advise you to use what you learn in this chapter to fix your map.

Ok, enough pre-amble. *Women henpeck men because their primary genetic imperative is not being met.*

To be more specific, women nag when their need for an alpha male is not being met.

This directive, as I already said, is the primary one and is emotionally the far more powerful and important one.

Think about all the men you have ever observed getting henpecked. Were they alpha or beta? They were beta--all of them.

Alpha males don't get nagged.

When a woman's need for an alpha is not getting met, she feels a tremendous unease and a creeping sense of dissatisfaction that she can't quite put her finger on.

The unmet need emotionally nags at her like an itch she cannot scratch. Women don't enjoy this feeling at all. In fact, it drives them completely crazy and they deal with it by nagging at you and finding fault with every little thing.

Contrary to popular belief, women don't enjoy the nagging or the arguing either.

The dominant and domineering woman that you see at grocery store is not behaving like that because she's a bully and wants to dominate. Women *hate* leading in a sexual relationship with their guy.

She's doing it because she resents having to step up, take the lead and dominate, and she's expressing her resentment at having to do so with a fit of impotent rage.

Women absolutely despise weakness in men. The only thing a woman despises more than weakness in a man is when the weakness is in the man she is with.

Weakness in men will *always* be punished by women. Lack of dominance and assertiveness in men will always be punished by women.

In addition, if a man is timid, then the woman's unhappiness about the unmet need of the first imperative is compounded by the fact that she's *rewarded* by being able to successfully bully her way to satisfaction of the second imperative (the economic imperative).

She can get him to buy her stuff and can more efficiently mine his financial resources with bullying behaviour, and now the problem becomes self-perpetuating.

All of a sudden the guy finds himself buying her flowers and chocolates or something else like a shopping trip or exotic holiday. He thinks that when he does this and she smiles and her heart melts, that means all is ok and he has solved the problem. But he hasn't; he's just bought himself a little time.

Instead, the sequence the relationship goes through looks like this (and it might be little familiar to you):

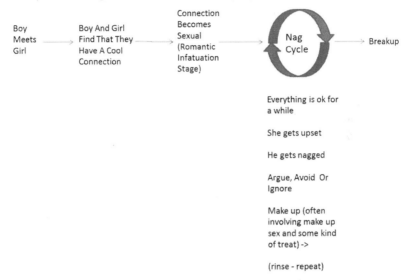

All the little things that make women feel their need for an alpha is not being met cause them to complain. But instead of telling their guy the real reason when he asks them what's wrong, they incorrectly identify the niggling little things as the source of the irritation.

This is why men don't get it. They think the insignificant things she's complaining about are the problem, because that's what they're being told.

Men can't work out why women are "so emotional," and get "so damn worked up over little things that mean nothing!"

I've never once in my life known of a woman who sat a guy down and politely explained to him that she's nagging him because her primary imperative is not being met.

The closest was when I observed a woman nagging her guy and telling him that he was "weak" and needed to "grow a pair of balls."

Anyway, the reason why women henpeck men and men don't rooster-peck women is those damn differing genetic imperatives again.

The henpecked man is not exclusively to blame for being henpecked, nor is the woman exclusively to blame. Like all such situations, this one takes two to create.

Essentially it's a mix of the unmet imperative of the female, and the unwillingness of the guy to "step up" that creates the problem.

If you are a guy and want to avoid being henpecked, what should you do? Learn how to be an alpha, which does not mean scream right back and hit your woman. Guys who are really alpha never "lose it" like that.

What I mean is: learn how to be a calm, confident guy who knows how to lead, to take care of business and to take care of your woman. That's what alphas do.

If you are a woman and you want to avoid the henpeck situation, find yourself an alpha.

That brings us neatly to the second way in which men and women drive each other crazy.

# 26 – Tame the Alpha (The Losing Game)

The normal and natural planes attract different types. Beta males are more drawn toward the normal sexual plane, whereas alpha males are drawn toward the natural.

The reasons for this should be fairly obvious. Since a beta male has fewer sexual options than an alpha, he will more highly regard the importance of fencing a female into an exclusivity agreement.

Alpha males, on the other hand, (who have more sexual options), gravitate to the natural plane and are far less concerned about fencing in a female.

Men will have the same biological imperative (having sex with lots of fertile women), regardless of whether they initially choose a fenced or an unfenced relationship, and regardless of whether they are alpha or beta.

Alpha males gravitating toward the natural plane and away from enforced monogamy provide a challenge that women find irresistible---this challenge is called "tame-the-alpha."

Beta males who are offering a woman what she claims she wants (security and a fenced relationship) are often confused by this dynamic and mistakenly think that they're offering women what they truly desire.

The confusion is clarified by understanding that the lure of being with an alpha, along with the challenge of tame-the-alpha, is what she really wants.

A beta offering a fenced relationship, outright and with no challenge, is offering neither of those things, and so is not offering her what she really wants.

If you've ever felt befuddled by why women go after bad boys and not nice guys, then wonder no more.

If you're a guy, don't misread the map at this point and think that it's about nice guys vs. bastards.

It's not; it's alpha vs. beta, which means strong, confident and dominant vs. weak and supplicating.

The confusion on people's maps is because bad boys or bastards exhibit more alpha characteristics and are not weak and supplicating--but don't let that confuse you.

Women don't enjoy being treated poorly, but at the same time they also despise weakness in men because that just goes directly against their primary imperative.

You can be strong and dominant without treating women poorly. You don't need to be a bastard to be an alpha.

## Why Tame-the-Alpha Is a Losing Game

Because alpha males have lots of options when it comes to women, and have the least interest in fencing or being fenced, female sexual company is not scarce but rather is abundant. Even if you get an alpha to agree to some kind of fenced relationship, this abundance is not going to change.

Apart from the fact that fencing him will crank up the jealousy and possessiveness in the relationship and invite the twin-headed monster to be a permanent guest who endlessly torments your emotions, the relationship has almost no chance of staying fenced and will become false-fenced.

This is a lose/lose proposition.

Fencing in an alpha guy will not change his nature or make him less desirable to other women—it will only make him more so. There's nothing more desirable in a man than the fact that other women find him desirable. Making him "unavailable" only increases his sexual market value.

What is the solution that will make him less attractive to other women? Why, convert him into a beta of course! Harp at him, nag at him to change, make him report to you on his location and what exact time he'll be home. Actually, make him account for *all* of his time, and nag him if he doesn't.

Make all the rules: no, of course he can't hang out with his buddies any more on a guy's night out. His buddies are likely to be other alphas, which means there are likely to be lots of other women around the group enjoying their company, and all kinds of flirting going on! That's not acceptable, and you have to make sure it doesn't happen!

Change him from a dominant guy to a submissive guy—just one more guy who misses the point of being a man. See the problem with that?

Yes, the woman is then in a fenced relationship with a beta male, which is exactly what she didn't want in the first place.

When women henpeck men because they're not getting their biological imperatives met, the loop goes like this:

Meet alpha -> successfully tame alpha -> covert alpha to beta -> feel bad about not being with an alpha -> complain that the man is not the man she fell in love with -> henpeck and feel miserable.

Of course the man in such a scenario will be almightily puzzled as to why a woman would be so hell-bent on changing him, and then when he's changed, endlessly complain to him that he's "not the man she fell in love with."

Lose/lose.

Playing tame-the-alpha is an exercise in self-abuse for women, played out at a subconscious level.

The only winning game to play with an alpha, and the only way to keep him, is to focus on having him in your life for the long term rather than keeping him in a fence.

Alpha men, contrary to popular female opinion, are both attainable and retainable as long as the woman is woman enough.

Obtaining an alpha man, getting into a fenced relationship with him and then just accepting that he cheats on you, is obviously pointless. If it's acceptable for the relationship to be unfenced, then it may as well be unfenced from the very beginning instead of becoming false-fenced later. At least that way there's no lying and deception.

In other words, the only strategy for women to use on an alpha that actually works is to maintain an unfenced relationship with him from the very beginning and be woman enough that he treats you as his queen bee.

This way he gets to stay alpha, which is what you loved about him in the first place, and the relationship cannot become false-fenced.

Win/win.

# 27 – Screwing Gays and Lesbians the Sex 2.0 Way

To put it mildly, the invention of Sex 2.0 totally screwed gays and lesbians--and not in a way they like being screwed.

If you look back through all of written and recorded history, back many thousands of years, you'll find occurrences of homosexuality and lesbianism throughout.

People have been homosexual forever, without any coercion or duress from society. In other words, being lesbian or gay is totally natural.

Yes, it's a minority percentage of the population, but most flowers that grow are not sunflowers--they are in a minority too. Does that mean sunflowers are unnatural? Of course not; if something grows or occurs naturally then it's natural.

That was just fine in a Sex 1.0 era because the natural sexual plane is all that existed; there was no concept of normal.

Then Sex 2.0 came along and the normal sexual plane arrived. This totally screwed gays and lesbians because (remember):

Natural = defined by nature and not by society

Normal = defined by society and not by nature

This means that, although homosexuality and lesbianism have always been totally natural by virtue of the fact that they occur naturally and without coercion, they later became "abnormal." Why? Society said so, and society defines the normal plane; not you or I or even nature defines it--society does.

The agenda of a Sex 2.0 society and the normal plane was all about heterosexual men and women grappling with the combination of PAC, property, babies and lines of heritage. These were of little concern to gays and lesbians, especially before the days of turkey basters and sperm banks.

As a result of the normal plane, lesbian women in a Sex 2.0 society are raised, under RD, to believe that their role as a woman is to become the sexual property of a man. Likewise, gay men are taught and pressured under RD to get married to a woman.

Both are marginalised and both suffer the stigma of being considered abnormal. They also suffer the stigma of being labelled "unnatural" by those too ignorant to grasp the conceptual difference between normal and natural.

Even if they tell their own parents about their sexual orientation, gays and lesbians commonly continue to receive RD from the parents' hope that they'll change.

Groupthink (which characterises Sex 2.0) dictates that those outside the group are immoral and wrong and must be shunned and persecuted.

Therefore, gays and lesbians are born into a world where they have no place on the normal plane, but instead receive all the hatred and discrimination that goes with it, including sometimes murderous violence.

This is a particularly pure and evil form of RD.

# 28 – Feminism Is Dead and How Feminists Killed It

Broadly speaking, there are two types of feminism based on two different map-reads of the word "equality."

The first says that women are as important as men and should not be treated as second-class citizens. I call this type one feminism, and it gave birth to such splendid movements as women's suffrage, in which women fought and died to bring to women all over the world the right to vote and the right to run for office.[xxviii]

Type one feminism must also be thanked for campaigning successfully for the political and social reform necessary to give women access to social mobility, jobs and careers, and their own financial security. Without this, the move to Sex 3.0 would not be possible.

Of course women should have the right to vote and equal access and opportunities in the workplace. Why? Because

**No authority of any kind has any legitimacy whatsoever unless it serves those who submit to it.**

It doesn't matter whether the authority is patriarchal, matriarchal, legal, economic or governmental.

Painful reminders of the problems of illegitimate authority happen on an almost daily basis. This book was written during the year of the Arab spring. 2011 was not a good year to be a dictator. Right now people are occupying Wall Street because they feel they have submitted to a system that has failed them and doesn't serve them.

As I type this today, there are reports on the news about protests in the streets of Egypt because the military wants to stipulate in the new constitution that they should be exempt from review and oversight by citizens. In other words, they want a free pass from the rule that governs the entire world:

**No authority of any kind has any legitimacy whatsoever unless it serves those who submit to it.**

Type one feminism was always bound to succeed because it is just. The battle for the vote and for social mobility and self-sufficiency for women has already been won in modern western society.

But in many countries of the world the battle is very far from won. Women in Saudi Arabia were only recently given the right to vote and stand in elections starting in 2015.

Clearly Saudi Arabia is much behind the West, but it's at least making improvements (although the announcement lost its shine when two days later a woman was sentenced to ten lashes for driving a car).

Women still are not legally allowed to drive in Saudi Arabia, and of course it's hard to achieve social mobility when you don't even have physical mobility.

The fight in countries such as this will go on, but the outcome will be the same for all of them eventually. Victory for type one feminism is inevitable, because

**No authority of any kind has any legitimacy whatsoever unless it serves those who submit to it.**

Not to recognise this is to misread the map.

So why do I say that feminism is dead? This brings me to the second map-read of the word "equality," which says that men and women are the same. I call this type two feminism.

Type two feminism insists that, apart from a few basic biological differences, gender roles are artificial social constructs propagated by men, who are considered to be the enemy or the oppressors.

Thinking of gender roles and biology as artificial social constructs is a self-delusion that can easily be addressed by watching a nature documentary.

Of course the best way to perpetuate self-delusion is to band into tightly-knit Aschian conformity cliques and wield shaming language against those who dare to disagree. That is what type two feminists do.

However, to perpetuate this self-delusion is to perpetuate the idea that the genetic imperatives themselves are artificial social constructs.

### Fog Alert

*Misogynist*

This word used to very specifically mean hatred of women.[xxix]

However, in modern society it's been hijacked by type two feminists to mean "you're not compliant with our agenda" or "you said something I disagree with on the subject of gender and now I feel irritated or angry."

Type two feminists might mistakenly label this book "misogynistic," but that assertion could now be viewed with the previous paragraph in mind.

Incidentally, the opposite of misogyny is misandry (the hatred of men). Ironically, many type two feminists are misandrists who indulge in the very thing they claim to decry--hatred of the opposite sex.[xxx]

## When Is A Double Standard Not A Double Standard?

When it's about two different things.

If a man sows his wild oats and sleeps around, he's labelled a stud. If a woman sleeps around she's labelled a slut. If you think that's a double standard, it's not. And if you think it's sexist, it's not that either.

### Fog Alert

*Sexist*

This word has been hijacked also and is now being used to mean any gender difference that women disapprove of or that makes them feel bad.

Sexism is about *seeing gender as relevant when it is not relevant,* and discriminating on that basis.[xxxi]

For example, men are taught not to hit women. Men are typically stronger and bigger than women and it's therefore not fair to hit them. Is this sexist? No, because physical size and strength *are* relevant when comparing men to women. The genders are clearly different in this regard.

One can't logically regard the slut/stud example as sexist but the "no hitting women" rule as not sexist just because one favours women and one doesn't. You can't have it both ways. Either both of them are sexist, or else neither is sexist.

As neither of these examples sees gender as *relevant when it is not* (gender clearly is relevant in both cases), then neither can be sexist. Sexism, again, is *seeing gender as relevant when it is not*.

The genetic imperatives of men and women are different because of a very basic difference in biology. From the previous information about genetic imperatives and how they play out in both Sex 1.0 and Sex 2.0, your map should reflect that.

A double standard is a double standard only when you apply two different standards to the same thing. Men and women are not the same thing. We are sexual polar opposites, like black and white, north and south, yin and yang. Not only are we sexual opposites, we have different genetic imperatives too.

Applying the same standards to both sexes--*where gender difference obviously applies*--does not make any sense.

*"The worst form of inequality is to try to make unequal things equal." – Aristotle*

The stud/slut example cannot be a double standard. If you thought it was, or if you thought it was sexist, then you were unduly influenced by type two feminism.

However, if you thought that it was unfair or unduly harsh toward women, then I agree with you completely. It's totally ridiculous and grossly unfair.

Luckily, I've already pointed out the solution to that problem. In a Sex 3.0 world there are no such things as sluts, and no such persecution. Later in the book we'll see why.

## False Flag

If you believe and are perpetuating the idea that the genetic imperatives themselves are artificial social constructs and that men are the enemy, you might be able to see at this point that the "enemy" really is nature itself.

Type two feminism fails both men and women. It fails women because it teaches them to give up their beauty and femininity, which is the very thing that gives them high value in the sexual marketplace. It fails men not only because unfeminine women are unattractive to them, but because the battle that type two feminists are waging is a "false flag operation."

A false flag operation is a military term used to deceive the public. The nature of the deception is that the hostilities appear as though they're being carried out by parties other than the real ones involved. Type two feminism is a false flag operation in that it claims the genetic imperatives supplied by nature are actually the evil inventions of men.

There never was a "battle of the sexes," because it is not type two feminists vs. men. The battle is type two feminists vs. nature.

The reason type one feminism succeeded is the same reason that type two feminism is already dead:

**No authority of any kind has any legitimacy whatsoever unless it serves those who submit to it.**

Regardless of whether a society is patriarchal, matriarchal or of any nature whatever, it has to serve the needs of everyone. Any authority has to serve both men and women.

*The betterment of both men and women should be the ultimate aim of any civilised society.*

This cannot be achieved by campaigning for the rights of 50% of the population at the expense of the other 50%.

The subjugation of either sex through patriarchy, matriarchy, radical feminism, physical violence, or through any other means is a failure of humanity. Life is not a zero sum game.

Type two feminism was nothing more than a war to eradicate gender.

They never had a chance of winning.

# 29 – Men and Women Cheat For Different Reasons

There is a funny story about former US president Calvin Coolidge which goes like this:

The President and Mrs Coolidge were being shown separately around an experimental government farm. When the first lady came to the chicken yard she noticed that a cockerel was mating with a hen very vigorously and with tremendous enthusiasm.

She gave an envious sigh, forlornly remembering the early days of her own marriage when the president was so enthusiastic. She asked the attendant how often the cockerel put on such a performance.

"Dozens of times each day," replied the attendant. The first lady smiled and said "tell that to the President when he comes by." A little later the President came by, and on being told, he asked "same hen every time?" The attendant replied "Oh no Mr President, a different hen every time" to which the president smiled and said "Tell that to Mrs Coolidge." [xxxii]

The Coolidge effect is an evolutionary biology term denoting a phenomenon that's been observed and scientifically documented in almost every living species of mammal, including us. [xxxiii]

The Coolidge effect essentially refers to the continued high level of sexual interest, enthusiasm and performance levels when new sexual partners are introduced.

It applies to both genders, although to a greater extent to males. The reason it applies more to males is obvious if you understand the differing genetic imperatives of men and women.

Men's genetic imperative dictates the need for variety. This of course is not a problem in unfenced relationships, but in fenced ones it often leads, sooner or later, to cheating.

Women like variety too, but at different periods of the relationship and for different reasons.

The more a woman is emotionally pair bonded, happy and "loved up," or otherwise romantically infatuated toward a man, the less attraction she will generally feel toward other men.

Men don't work like this. Since the male biological imperative is to have sex with lots of women, the sexual attraction men feel towards other women remains fairly constant even if they don't act on it.

For women, infatuation with a man = lack of attraction to other men

For men, infatuation with a woman = infatuation with a woman

A man's level of attraction to women will continue to correlate closely to the levels of youth, beauty, fertility and attractiveness of the women.

Whether or not a man acts on that attraction is another matter entirely. If he is in a fenced relationship, it depends on his core values, his level of fear about getting caught and what he has to lose, and guilt over breaking the fenced agreement. What it comes down to is whether those considerations outweigh the desire.

The nature of male attraction is very important for women to understand. A woman often makes the totally incorrect "He doesn't not love me any more" assumption when she observes her man looking at or displaying signs of attraction toward other women.

To get hurt by or angry at a man who turns his head when he walks past a girl in the street who is clearly a head-turner in the fertility and attractiveness department is insanity, because it's being hurt and angry at the biological imperative itself.

Let him look; it doesn't mean he doesn't love you any more. Remember that without the genetic imperatives humanity would lack its tenaciously high ability to survive, and the woman who's feeling hurt and offended wouldn't even have been born.

A man can be a devoted and loving partner who wants to climb mountains, conquer kingdoms and write tender love songs for a woman---and still find signs of youth, beauty and fertility in other women attractive.

*His desire to look is completely unrelated to his feelings for you.*

We've already seen that women's biological imperative evolved and changed during the evolution from Sex 1.0 to Sex 2.0. This change happened because it needed to. Men's biological imperative, on the other hand, did not change at all with Sex 2.0, because it didn't need to.

The lack of change is not because men are slow. It's just that no evolutionary advantage was offered that would make a change desirable or necessary.

Women who don't understand this tend to use phrases like "men are such dogs" when they observe male behaviour. I think of such women as suffering from canine syndrome.

Men are not dogs. Men are men.

Women suffering from canine syndrome, and whose partners cheat, are also likely to feel and to say things like, "He never really truly loved me," or "This proves that he never really cared." This is a faulty map reading.

The faulty map reading causes the thinking that goes like this:

*I know I would never cheat on someone I truly loved. He cheated on me. Therefore he never truly loved me.*

Men who do love their partner but are not able to go against nature (i.e. resist their biological imperative) often find themselves in a fundamentally confusing situation. They totally understand the anger and hurt that's been caused, but can't understand why their very solid prior history of loving and caring behaviour is so categorically written off as false or worthless.

This "He never really loved me" assumption is just the projection of female psycho-sexuality onto men. This happens because people assume that the biological imperatives are the same for men and women. As we've seen, they are not.

A 1985 study by Drs. Shirley Glass and Thomas Wright found that in cases of marital infidelity, the majority of unfaithful men (56%) rated the marriage either "happy" or "very happy." Of unfaithful women, however, only 36% rated the marriage "happy" or "very happy." [xxxiv]

Men's need for variety and the unfamiliar is a genetic imperative. In fact, that's their only genetic imperative.

Incidentally, if anyone reading this book is thinking that its male author is somehow attempting to rationalise male infidelity in order to excuse it, full disclosure for the sake of clarity is in order.

First, I've never been married and have no intention of ever getting married, so cheating on my wife was and is not possible, nor will it be possible in the future.

Second, I engage exclusively in unfenced relationships, and everyone who knows me knows this. (Remember that unfenced doesn't necessarily mean more than one sexual partner at a time, it means no enforced monogamy and no fence to hop over while the other isn't looking.) In short, it's completely impossible for me to cheat on anyone.

I am not saying this to try to claim the moral high ground. I have had false-fenced relationships in the past. I am just saying this to make clear that I have no self-justification agenda.

Nor am I suggesting that, although cheating and the reasons for it are understandable, it's fine and OK if people do it. Cheating is not OK because it goes against *all* of the four pillars of pure form relationships. Again, these pillars are communication, honesty, trust and respect, and any relationship that aspires to high functionality should be built on them.

Many women understandably feel that men's need for variety and unfamiliarity is unconscionable, because it goes against their historical need for security in the long term.

However, the sexes could decide to call it evens because women developed a strategy in the Sex 2.0 marketplace which men find unconscionable.

## Who's The Daddy?

Since the female genetic imperative is:

> 1 - Seek high quality alpha male DNA and physical protection and security for both self and child (socio)

2 - Seek a partner who can provide financial security for self and children. Prevent other women from diluting such arrangement (economic).

And since the game of "tame the alpha" is such a difficult one for women, a far more attainable goal for satisfying the second imperative is to tame a beta.

Once the beta is tamed, however, the primary imperative still needs satisfying. The nagging dissatisfaction a woman often has with her beta is frequently dealt with by … well … by nagging him, and by having extra marital trysts with an alpha.

Women, usually subconsciously, feel the urge for this bit on the side most strongly during ovulation--the fertile part of their cycle. As a result, there are an awful lot of children in the world whose "daddy" is not their daddy.

Surveys on the exact percentage vary, due to the social difficulties of attempting to get honest answers on a mass scale. However, several 1970s studies in both the north and south of England found the percentages to be in the range of 20-30% [xxxv]

The evolutionary purpose behind "cuckolding" is rooted in women's desires that their children have both strong alpha DNA and strong financial stability. Whilst men may find this unconscionable, it makes perfect sense on a biological level. The genetic imperatives are nothing more than the most efficient DNA survival strategy for both women and their offspring.

At some level men of course know this, which is why female virginity has historically been a highly-prized asset in the Sex 2.0 marketplace. And once the prize is owned, a man knows that fencing in her sexuality and vigilantly patrolling the fence is his best chance of not being cuckolded into raising someone else's child as his own.

## Women Are Just As Unfaithful As Men

If you want to seize on my assertion earlier that "female infatuation for a man = lack of attraction to other men" as evidence that women are naturally monogamous or *more* monogamous than men, then remember that I said female *infatuation*.

In the five steps from the chapter "Jealousy and Possessiveness," you may recall that infatuation is just one stage of the five-step twin-headed monster sequence. It's stage three, and it's followed by the spin cycle phase (usually the longest phase of a relationship), and then the breakup.

There is no phase of a relationship in which women are less likely to cheat than in the infatuation stage. The giddy happiness experienced then is like glue that keeps her stuck to one man. This leads many men and women to theorise (incorrectly) that women are naturally the more monogamous sex, or that women are less likely to cheat (i.e. more likely to be loyal).

How long the infatuation stage of a long-term relationship lasts varies from person to person, and can also vary depending on other factors like geographic distance and how often you see each other.

Being together 24/7, dealing with life's dreary and unromantic details like paying bills and who should do the dishes, makes infatuation wear off faster. The infatuation stage can be anything from a few months to, at most, one or two years.

Women who've been married for at least four years are far more likely to cheat than women who are just months into a fresh relationship with a partner they're romantically infatuated with. [xxxvi]

Practically all female infidelity in relationships happens during the spin cycle or the nag cycle stages. Starting an affair as a way of prompting a breakup is also very common.

However, as I said in the chapter where I covered the twin-headed monster sequence, not all relationships follow this pattern. It's just the most common one, which is why it merited its own chapter.

So let's take a look at some other relationship killers that can cause men and women to seek lovers elsewhere.

## Stagnation by Exclusivity

Complacency is a big relationship killer. Nothing's more likely to make a couple mutually complacent than being granted 24/7 access to each other.

Again, the genetic imperatives dictate that men's role is to entice women into sex, and women's role is to entice men into commitment. So once commitment is guaranteed regardless of how badly she treats him, the man has removed the main incentive for her to make an effort. The result can be complacence.

She doesn't dress sexily or go out of her way any more. She maybe gains weight, hangs out in sweat pants and takes no care of her looks. The "use sex to entice commitment" dynamic unavoidably shifts.

Maybe she used to wake him up with a blowjob every morning, but now she doesn't like to do that any more.

On the male side of the equation, once a man knows he has a guaranteed sex partner (nominally at least) at home waiting for him every night, he can slack off in the commitment department. He can get away with spending more time out drinking with his male friends or more time at the office.

If she has a job too she'll often spend more time at the office, so now they can blame their dwindling sex life on their busy careers.

He too can get away with making no effort-- sitting on the couch drinking beer, farting and belching his way through the football game, paying little attention to her, and spending more time playing video games.

He can lose his alpha edge (if he had one), and live the life of the domesticated beta. This leaves her to wonder what happened to the man she fell in love with.

I call this the stagnation by exclusivity effect.

Couples often find that mating in captivity is not as desirable as they thought it would be. Their belief that love conquers all does not solve the problem.

Not only do such couples feel complacent and bored and take each other for granted, but an underlying feeling of mutual resentment about their dull sex life is also not unusual.

The result is that neither party is happy, and both parties may feel justifiably tempted to seek an affair.

## Familiarity

When a couple has been together for a long time, it's not uncommon for them to develop a level of familiarity with each other that reflects the root meaning of the word--"like family."

This results in one or both partners developing a more brotherly or sisterly kind of loving relationship with each other, rather than being lovers.

They see each other as family because mommy or daddy is the one who looked after and provided for them when they were growing up, and those are the roles they're now playing for each other.

Although deeply concerned with the wellbeing of the other, couples in this situation often cheat because they both need sex and they find that their relationship suffers from an inevitable wane of sexual desire for each other.

Early on in the relationship she might not have cared at all if, in the throes of passion, he tore her clothes off--even if her favourite blouse gets ripped. Now not only does she find the idea of sex a bit weird and like having sex with her brother, but she gets a bit annoyed even being kissed by her partner if it smudges her makeup.

The pattern of sex a couple of times every time they saw each other when they first started dating wanes to a couple of times a week, then a few times a month, and then hardly ever. The sex life then consists of visits to a relationship counsellor for advice on how to get the spark back.

"Family" couples are not the only ones looking for advice on how to get the spark back. Those suffering from stagnation by exclusivity often look for the same advice, so here is my unconventional take on it.

## How to Get the Spark Back

Cosmo magazine won't tell you how to get the spark back, and neither will a marriage guidance counsellor, but I will.

My advice is to rely on the Coolidge effect, which is to continue high levels of sexual interest, enthusiasm and performance by introducing new sexual partners.

To get the spark back, unfence the relationship. Spending the GDP of a small developing nation on sexy lingerie for you or your partner like Cosmo told you to ain't gonna do it.

How to never lose the spark in the first place? Keep the relationship unfenced from the very beginning.

The problem with this advice is not that it's bad; the Coolidge effect has already been scientifically documented in human beings (both men and women).

The problem is twofold. First, introducing new partners is not a realistic option in a fenced relationship if you haven't killed the twin-headed monster. Second, keeping the relationship unfenced from the very beginning is not really an option that society offers you in a Sex 2.0 world. But I have some good news:

Sex 2.0 is dying.

# 30 – The Breakdown of the Sex 2.0 Deal

To review:

When raised in a Sex 2.0 society, men and women are taught these roles:

Women are taught their entire lives that they have to sell their sexuality in exchange for security—ultimately, the security of marriage to a man.

Men are taught that, if they want a long term sexual relationship, they must put a woman's sexuality into a box, slam the lid, and stamp and label the box as their property.

Those are the two sides of the deal.

In modern Western society women these days have access to social mobility. In other words, women can now have jobs, careers and their own money. They can provide themselves with security, and do not need to sell their sexuality to a man (i.e. get married) to get it.

Therefore women's side of the Sex 2.0 deal has already broken down.

On the other side of the deal, essentially men are told that they have to make a woman's sexuality their property in order to have any chance of reliably establishing lines of heritage.

But in modern society we already have technology that can easily determine paternity with greater than 99.9% accuracy at the DNA level. This establishes lines of heritage much more reliably than does the system of legally handcuffing couples to each other in marriage.

Marriage combined with fencing in her sexuality and policing the fence with jealousy and possessiveness probably provides only 80% accuracy at best. This seems like a lot more hassle and a far inferior result, so why do it? [xxxvii]

Watson and Crick first mapped DNA in England only in 1953. Paternity testing at the DNA level has been around only since 1984 when Sir Alec Jeffreys invented it, and it became available for use only in 1988. (Prior to that paternity was tested using blood typing, which was less accurate.) The home testing kit, which brought widespread testing availability (at least in the Western world), didn't come until very recently-- the late nineties. [xxxviii]

So the technology behind our ability to buy a test kit for less than 100 pounds, dollars or euros and test ourselves at home using simple cheek swabs evolved only in the last couple of decades, whereas the Sex 2.0 dynamic evolved over thousands and thousands of years.

If the whole of human history was shrunk to a single 24-hour day, with the present moment being midnight, DNA testing and social mobility for women both arrived at a tiny fraction of one second before the stroke of midnight—barely the blink of an eye.

## The Two Lies

Over many thousands of years, human sexuality has evolved based on the conviction that sexual fidelity and enforced lifetime monogamy for women were the only ways a man could feel reasonably confident that his children were his own and that his heirs were legitimate.

Therefore, modern day human sexuality evolved from the acceptance of two lies, one of which used to be true but is not true any more, and one of which was never true in the first place.

> 1 - To best ensure parental lineage, men have to make women sexual property

> 2 - Women cannot be trusted

The first one used to be true but is not true any more.

The second one was never true to begin with. Women can be trusted. They can be trusted to act like women and to follow their genetic imperative, just as men can be trusted to act like men and to follow theirs.

So, with the invention of simple home-based paternity testing kits, men's side of the Sex 2.0 deal has broken down too.

Conclusion? The Sex 2.0 deal is no longer valid simply because it is no longer relevant, certainly not in modern western society anyway. Both sides of the deal have broken down.

So if the deal is no longer valid, why do people still follow it?

Well, human sexuality evolves very, very slowly, which means that we have not caught up with the present-day facts.

Women are still raised to believe that they have to sell their sexuality in exchange for security to a man (ultimately in marriage) even though they can provide their own security.

Men still believe that they have to provide said security and have to fence in a woman's sexuality in order to allay paternity concern.

Human sexuality in the modern age is like a car crunching gears in its attempt to switch from Sex 2.0 to Sex 3.0.

There are several significant reasons why, and we'll look at them in the next chapters.

# 31 – Twelve Angry Monkeys

Once upon a time there was a huge monkey forest where a large band of monkeys roamed free. They swung from branches freely, played around in the shallow waters, and although food and monkey business were occasionally squabbled over, they were free and happy in their natural environment.

That is, they were free and happy until one day everything changed. Twelve unlucky monkeys were drugged and captured!

The group of 12 adults (six male and six female) dozily woke up again a few hours later to find themselves in a large metal box. It was not a cage as such, since there were no bars to climb or swing on. The box was totally smooth on the inside.

The only light that came into the box was through an open skylight. They could see their natural habitat clearly through it, but the ceiling was far too high for even the biggest monkey to jump and reach.

Then one of the bigger adult monkeys saw a metal chain hanging down from the skylight. It was quite high up but he realised that if he jumped really hard he could grab it and climb. Freedom!

He ran and jumped as hard as he could, grabbed the end of the chain, and started climbing excitedly up toward freedom as fast as he could. Then something happened.

The metal chain was electrified, and the monkey got a sharp, painful electric shock that made him fall back to the ground. Not only that, but at the same time the entire cage became electrified and all the other monkeys all got shocked too.

Another adult monkey tried to climb to his freedom a little later with the same result, and again all 12 monkeys got shocked.

After a few attempts the monkeys learned that trying to climb the metal chain meant everyone got nasty shocks, so they didn't try it again.

They all soon realised that the chain was electrified 24/7, since the background buzz of electricity could quite clearly be heard if they walked anywhere near the chain. It was a sound that never went away, day or night.

So they resigned themselves to their fate of living in the cage. It was not a very nice cage because there wasn't much to play with. There was a big cardboard box filled with handcuffs and handcuff keys in the corner of the cage, but what fun was that? What would the monkeys want with those? They were used to being free. Being trapped in a cage was bad enough for freedom-loving monkeys, so the handcuffs and keys went untouched.

Occasionally their captors would drop some bananas through the skylight, and there was a running tap in another corner for fresh water, so the monkeys were able to survive even though the air was not nice and fresh like outside and there was nothing to swing on.

Some monkeys beat their fists against the metal walls, but that was no use. Nobody ever escaped so they stopped trying and went back to their usual routine of eating and making monkey business and squabbling over who was the alpha male and who got first choice of the food and the females.

A few of the 12 monkeys became philosophical and religious about their fate. They took to gathering in one corner of the cage so they could discuss amongst themselves whether a great invisible sky-god monkey was somehow punishing them for some sins they had committed, and if so, *what* could those sins possibly be and how might they appease him?

After a week one of the adult female monkeys was replaced with a new adult female. This new monkey saw the metal chain and made for her escape. The other monkeys, not wanting to be shocked, leapt on her and beat her up before she could even reach the chain. The new monkey attempted to go for the chain a few more times before learning that going for the chain means that other monkeys will beat her up.

Still not realising why the other monkeys were beating her up, she developed a crafty plan. She waited until all the other monkeys were asleep and then tried to escape under cover of darkness!

Of course she got electrocuted in the middle of the night and the other 11 monkeys realised that the only thing they hate more than getting the electric shock is to be woken up from sleep by it. The monkeys became even angrier.

One of the monkeys came up with an idea. He grabbed a set of handcuffs and handcuffed himself to the new monkey to stop her trying to pull the same trick again whilst they were asleep (and also because he thought she was quite cute).

The religious monkeys declared that this was a sign from the great invisible sky-god monkey himself that all the monkeys must choose one partner and handcuff themselves to their partner; they also declared that any monkey who didn't would go to monkey hell.

The monkeys shrugged and even the ones who didn't actually believe in the invisible sky-god monkey decided to go along with it for the sake of a peaceful life and because it would make it easier to stop other newly-introduced monkeys from waking them up in the middle of the night with nasty electric shocks.

Besides, what if they were wrong and found out too late that monkey hell does really exist! They did not want to go there if it really existed (which they seriously doubted it did).

And so all the adult monkeys handcuffed themselves to their most preferred monkey business partner (with the alpha males getting first pick) and made baby monkeys with them.

The adult monkeys agreed to wait until the baby monkeys were almost grown up enough to be able to reach the metal chain before handcuffing them to someone.

There were some brief squabbles between some of the adult monkeys as to whether the parents of the baby monkey should get to choose who their baby got handcuffed to when they grew up or if the baby would get to choose for themselves when the time came.

They could not come to an agreement on that one, but they agreed that as long as everyone got handcuffed to a partner when they grew old enough, things would be ok.

Every week like clockwork, one of the adult monkeys got replaced by a new adult monkey (sometimes a male for a male and sometimes a female for a female), and the departing monkey would leave their descendants behind.

Because this happened so regularly, the new adult monkeys were soon being met by a welcoming committee and taught not to grab the metal chain, and to handcuff themselves to a partner. They learned that failure to comply with either rule would make the invisible sky-god monkey very angry indeed, and that he would send them to monkey hell.

Gradually over time, all of the original adult monkeys were replaced and none of their descendants were old enough to *ever* have received an electric shock from anybody grabbing the metal chain. This meant that, for the first time…

### None of the monkeys in the cage had ever received an electric shock.

Gradually the causal connection between grabbing the chain and receiving electric shocks was lost, because no one left had ever received one or talked to anyone who ever had.

However, none of the monkeys wished to offend anyone else in the group by tarnishing the ancient teachings of the original 12 wise monkeys, nor to anger the great invisible sky-god monkey and go to monkey hell (which by now everyone was convinced was a barren, miserable place completely without bananas).

Everybody by this stage was a religious monkey, and they all took to pondering about the great question of the "outside"--- this place that the 12 wise monkeys called "nature" beyond the skylight. All agreed that it must be a wicked place without morals and correct rules and that only those on the inside were morally correct.

At this stage, the monkeys' captors brought the experiment to an end, switched off the current that electrified the cage and the metal chain, and left the facility.

One of the monkeys standing near the metal chain noticed that the buzzing sound of electricity had stopped, but decided not to say anything to the other monkeys. There was no point. He knew and everyone knew that touching the chain was forbidden. It would only make the group and the great invisible sky-god monkey angry. Anyway, those on the outside in "nature" were immoral beasts that lived in a world where proper and correct rules were not followed.

Anyway, pretty soon everyone in the group was far more concerned about another matter entirely. After several days without captors to bring food, the poor monkeys began to starve.

Although free to leave and return to nature, they remained handcuffed to each other in the knowledge that they were morally correct and that "nature" was a wicked place for those without morals.

The lack of bananas caused them to wonder if they had already been sent to monkey hell by the great invisible sky-god monkey. What sin had they committed now? Some religious monkeys decided that all monkeys must have been born with original sin. That was the only possible explanation.

Since the captors had left the facility, other monkeys in the outside world felt safe to approach the area around the facility once more, and they began to make the area their own again.

A rogue monkey in the outside world was out one day happily collecting bananas when he climbed onto the roof and peered into the skylight. He was amazed by what he saw.

He was greeted by the sight of dozens of emaciated monkeys, with a metal chain dangling from the celling offering them an easy way to escape. Being rather puzzled, he swung down, bananas in hand, to find out what was going on.

Of course all the monkeys gasped when they saw him touch the metal chain and swing down onto the floor. You are not supposed to touch the metal chain, they thought! Everybody knows that!

The rogue monkey, on taking a closer look at the emaciated monkeys and noticing that they were all handcuffed to each other said, "There is loads of food out there. That's your natural habitat too! Are you crazy? What they hell are you doing in here all handcuffed to each other and starving, especially when you have such an easy way to escape?"

As none of the remaining monkeys had any causal link between the metal chain and receiving electric shocks, they all angrily waved their fist in the air in unison and shouted the only thing they could think of:

"THAT'S JUST THEY WAY WE DO THINGS AROUND HERE!"

The rogue monkey shrugged his shoulders and scampered back up the metal chain and through the skylight into nature, before they could even blink.

The descendants of the 12 original monkeys looked on in astonishment. They had never seen a monkey do that before, and in their weak, handcuffed and surprised state, they hadn't even had time to stop the rogue monkey before he did it.

As they pondered the astonishing thing they had seen, the elder monkeys and the religious leader monkeys expressed outrage about the actions of the rogue monkey. They told themselves that they knew all along that nature was immoral. The fact that the rogue monkey so casually did the unthinkable and climbed the metal chain, not once but twice, only proved it!

Meanwhile, the hungry eyes of some of the other monkeys drifted towards the cardboard box in the corner, and they started to wonder which one of the keys inside would unlock their handcuffs.

# 32 – Groupthink and the Breakdown of the Sex 2.0 Deal

The monkey story is a fable about how groupthink works.

Let's go through Irving Janis's eight symptoms of groupthink in light of the collapse of the Sex 2.0 deal. (Underlined text is Janis's.) [xxxix]

## 1 - Illusion of invulnerability –Creates excessive optimism.

Doing things because "that's just the way we do things around here" is just that.

It's a state of optimistic self-denial that insists that "this must be right because this is the way we have always done things" and the entire group agrees on it. The decisions of the group therefore must be bullet proof and totally correct.

Both monkey and man are guilty of this.

## 2 - Collective rationalization – Members discount information and do not reconsider their assumptions.

The collapse of the reasons behind the Sex 2.0 deal, as symbolised by the electric shocks being turned off for the monkeys, has not caused mankind to reconsider its assumptions about marriage, nor to think about living more in tune with nature. In the same way, the monkeys don't reconsider their assumptions about climbing the chain and escaping back to nature, nor the wisdom of handcuffing themselves to each other.

The monkeys no longer had reason to wear the handcuffs; it became a thing of the past just as mankind's original reason for inventing marriage and handcuffing ourselves to each other became a thing of the past with the collapse of the Sex 2.0 deal.

The monkeys forgot the causal reasons for coming up with their rules just as we forgot the causal reasons for coming up with the Sex 2.0 deal and inventing marriage in the first place.

The monkeys' reason for not touching the chain (electric shock) had been switched off, but because they had long forgotten the causal reasons for group policy about it, they still went along with it. Similarly, we still go along with the Sex 2.0 deal.

### 3 - Belief in inherent morality – Members believe in the rightness of their cause.

After a while the monkeys developed a belief that their way of life and their rules were the only morally correct ones and that nature and everything outside was "immoral." Many human beings believe that respecting and following our natural genetic imperatives is immoral.

The belief of some people that they occupy the moral high ground is a way of dealing with their fear that their map is wrong. Labelling everything and everyone outside as immoral externalises that fear and makes them avoid change and cling desperately to their maps.

This is one of the big reasons why the decline in marriage in modern Western society is not causing a significant debate about the way forward--just a large amount of hand-wringing about the "decline of moral standards."

This is classic groupthink.

**4 - Stereotyped views of out-groups – Negative views of the "enemy" make effective responses to conflict seem unnecessary.**

That's why in a Sex 2.0 world we have concepts of some women as immoral sluts and whores. These women fall outside of the Sex 2.0 deal, and everything outside the Sex 2.0 deal must by definition be immoral.

It must be stigmatised, demonised and despised.

However, women who sell their sexuality in exchange for security (rather than cash), however, fall *within* the Sex 2.0 deal and are therefore moral, right, proper and just.

Likewise, this book will be thought of immoral by many for the very same reasons that the monkeys thought that nature was immoral. This will be the case even though I am not condemning marriage at all and am only condemning self-deception.

**5 - Direct pressure on dissenters – Members are under pressure not to express arguments against any of the group's views.**

Just as the monkeys who did not believe in the great invisible sky-god monkey went along with the groupthink for the sake of an easy life, the weekly new arrivals were met with a welcoming committee who taught them the rules - the easy way or the hard way.

Human beings do this too when it comes to sexual relationships. It's called relationship duress.

**6 - Self-censorship – Doubts and deviations from the perceived group consensus are not expressed.**

After the electric current was switched off, none of the monkeys wished to offend anyone else in the group by tarnishing the ancient teachings of the original 12 wise monkeys, nor to anger the great invisible sky-god monkey.

As for human beings, when it comes to sexual relationships, we dare not step outside the group consensus for fear of disapproval, of being regarded as wrong, deviant or immoral, or of being subject to relationship duress.

This is rooted in ancient tribal thinking and fear of being thrown out of the tribe.

7 - Illusion of unanimity – The majority view and judgments are assumed to be unanimous.

This will always be assumed if doubts are not expressed and if people are afraid to act on the basis of new information out of fear of disrupting group harmony.

8 - Self-appointed 'mind guards' – Members protect the group and the leader from information that is problematic or contradictory to the group's cohesiveness, view, and/or decisions.

"One of the monkeys standing near the metal chain noticed that the buzzing sound of electricity had stopped, but decided not to say anything to the other monkeys. There was no point. He knew and everyone knew that touching the chain was forbidden. It would only make the group and the great invisible sky-god monkey angry."

Humans do this; the clergy do this professionally.

We have mental guards constantly telling ourselves collectively that marriage is absolutely the right thing, even though we have not done it for most of human history and only started doing it very recently.

## Who Are You?

In the fable of the 12 monkeys, who are you?

You are very probably a descendant of the 12 angry monkeys, meaning that you grew up in a Sex 2.0 cage.

Do you want to stay in the cage or do you want to follow the rogue monkey?

If you want to stay in the cage, I can't help you any more. We are at the end of the Sex 2.0 section of the book and you don't really need a map for territory you are not going to explore.

Maybe you want to follow the rogue monkey but you like the idea of being handcuffed to your beloved because of the comfort that brings you. Please--bring the handcuffs with you and come along. You can still use them in a Sex 3.0 world if you want to.

Maybe you don't need the handcuffs and you just want to follow the rogue monkey. Maybe you even want to *be* the rogue monkey.

It does not matter, as long as you are heading for that skylight; these next chapters are for you.

# 33 – R.I.P. Sex 2.0

The Sex 2.0 deal was the best human beings could come up with at the time, but it contained a number of fundamental flaws including, but not limited to:

**1 - Sex 2.0 schism**---Two planes of human sexuality, the "natural" and the "normal," started operating at the same time, which allowed us to come up with all kinds of things to contradict ourselves and our nature.

A set of social imperatives that contradicts our genetic imperatives=fail.

**2 - No Guarantees** - The entire purpose of the Sex 2.0 deal was to ease male insecurity by guaranteeing the paternity of the children and perpetuation of their genes and lines of heritage.

The Sex 2.0 deal does not guarantee any of those things; it was merely the best chance. Again: fail.

**3 - Relationship duress** - Because there are no guarantees, the invention of relationship duress became necessary as an additional insurance policy.

Relationship duress is a very serious problem that causes all kinds of mapping errors to be passed on like viruses, creates unrealistic viewpoints and expectations, and makes it only more difficult to navigate the terrain and have success in relationships.

Also, we have to labour under RD our entire lives – even if we get married! Epic fail.

**4 - Jealousy and possessiveness** – Particularly the creation of the twin-headed monster—jealousy and possessiveness, but also stagnation by exclusivity and familiarity, cause untold human misery every single day. These global miseries include pandemic violence, domestic abuse and murder.

Even those relationships that avoid physical violence tend to follow an extremely predictable five-step sequence, resulting in the termination of otherwise healthy relationships, and the loss—forever—of valuable human connections. Epic fail.

**5 - No Monogamy Anyway** – Despite all of the above, and despite socially-mandated and RD-enforced monogamy, human beings still did not become monogamous!

In every single human civilization ever studied where monogamy was enforced, infidelity was discovered--even in the ones where the penalty for infidelity is death.

What kind of creature *needs* the threat and penalty of death just to go along with its own nature? None.

The fact that all cultures where infidelity was punished by death saw documented cases of infidelity anyway tells you that *we are not naturally monogamous*.

Human beings never have been monogamous, are not now, and are not likely to become so in the millennia to come. One wonders *why* we go to so much effort to makes ourselves so miserable. Yet another epic fail.

## Tipping Point

Ladies and gents, we have reached tipping point. The Sex 2.0 deal is already obsolete and the Sex 2.0 world as a whole is currently undergoing a cascading failure.

That means that failure in one part of the system causes a failure in another part of the system, which causes a failure somewhere else, and so on. Failures ripple out until you end up with a large-scale cascading failure, like the collapse of a huge dam that began with a small water leak.

In the case of Sex 2.0, this is actually a very good thing.

Seriously, if Sex 2.0 was submitted by even a junior college student as a suggested blueprint for all human sexual relationships in the modern era as part of a college project, it would get an F.

It's only groupthink that keeps us from realising the failure, because the failure has been staring us in the face for quite some time now.

*"The hardest thing to explain is the glaringly evident which everybody has decided not to see." - Ayn Rand*

Ok, so it's time to say…

## R.I.P. Sex 2.0 – A Eulogy

It's always difficult to say goodbye to an old and faithful loved one, but we are gathered here today to do just that and to pay our final respects.

Sex 2.0 lived a long life, nigh on 10,000 years. As a small child he wandered the lands of Asia and the Middle East, going wherever property and farming were. He loved those two things more than anything else.

His prominence rose and his domination spread slowly but surely. He was always determined, and this determination allowed him to eventually conquer the whole world! He even conquered the mighty USA, by arriving on the boats that brought the first Europeans there all those hundreds of years ago.

It is noted with some irony that Sex 2.0 was finally stricken down and killed off by the very same two things that killed off his father, Sex 1.0 - a social breakthrough and a technological breakthrough.

In the case of Sex 1.0, the social breakthrough was the invention of property and the technological breakthrough was the invention of rudimentary farm tools like shovels, picks, ploughs, etc. that seem primitive now but were cutting-edge technology at the time. People became farmers and invented property and marriage, and those things finished off Sex 1.0.

With Sex 2.0, the social breakthrough was women's access to social mobility and financial security, combined with the physical security provided by police, jails and the court system.

The first technological breakthrough that dealt Sex 2.0 a bitter blow was the invention of the pill, which drastically reduced the need for women to entice men into commitment in order to have sex.

We recall Sex 2.0's frequent and often drunken laments about the good old days of the 18th century. Back then, without reliable contraceptives or the welfare state, the options for women in regard to being sexual were: find a husband, starve to death or become a prostitute.

Yes, the years before the pill and the welfare state were his golden years, and he lived them well. Since then, his adversaries dealt him many blows and weakened him for sure.

Toward the end, Sex 2.0 was quite weak and frail. The invention of DNA paternity testing was the straw that broke the camel's back. Testing could determine paternity with more than 99.9% accuracy, which was far better than he could ever determine it. And so he passed away into obsolescence--gone but never to be forgotten.

There is apt symmetry in the fact that Sex 2.0 was killed off by the products of the modern technological revolution, while his father before him was killed off by the agricultural revolution.

May he rest in peace.

## Right Hardware, Wrong Software

One of the very serious problems Sex 2.0 always presented is that (to use a computer metaphor) our hardware (our DNA and our biological nature) is not wired to be monogamous, and yet society runs software (Sex 2.0) that tells us we have to be monogamous.

In other words, we are running software that is *really not very compatible* with the hardware. Kind of a problem, don't you think?

Maybe it's time for a upgrade.

# 34 – Sex 3.0

## *Sex 3.0 Duration – The present day forward*

In this and the next few chapters we'll look at the core principles of Sex 3.0, and at how these eradicate or alleviate some of the problems of Sex 2.0

After that, we'll take a look at the Sex 3.0 marketplace.

First let's get rid of any idea you might have that by going through the skylight and following the rogue monkey you will wander off into some kind of utopian land of the author's crazy imagination.

There is no going back to a fictional rose-tinted version of the Sex 1.0 era where everyone lives in hippie communes and dances around campfires naked with flowers in their hair, and where it would be considered rude for a woman not to give a random passing fella a complimentary blowjob as a way of saying "hello."

The first thing to realise about moving forward is that there's no going back to Sex 1.0

The reason why is that you cannot uninvent property. It doesn't matter how much you might want that—it's not gonna happen.

The good news though is that you do get to return to nature in Sex 3.0, but only if you want to. In other words, Sex 3.0 is a choice.

## Laying the Cards on the Table

The first big difference you will notice relates to honesty. To put it bluntly:

Sex 2.0 = Dishonest

Sex 3.0 = Honest

From the very beginning of Sex 3.0, the two cards are laid on the table in plain view, and under no duress whatsoever, you get to choose.

In a Sex 2.0 world you are never really offered the choice at the beginning of a relationship. You certainly are not offered that by society anyway. The normal plane with its fenced relationships is shoved in your face your entire life, and the choice of the natural plane and unfenced relationships is dishonesty hidden from you.

If the two planes of human sexuality were those coasters on the table in front of you right now, society would have its left hand over the "natural" one, its right hand shoving the "normal" one in your face whilst tapping it with his finger and the conversation might go like this:

**Society** (holding the normal one up to your face): Choose this! Choose this! (tap tap). You have to choose this! (tap tap)

**You**: What's that?

**Society**: What's what?

**You**: That thing under your left hand, the other hand?

**Society** (slipping into used car salesman mode): Oh that? Oh that's nothing!

**You**: Well, it's not nothing or you wouldn't be hiding it from me, would you? What is it?

**Society**: Oh that? I did not see that there before actually. Oh that's nothing really. That's just the natural sexual plane. That's just a bunch of … you know …. casual sex and stuff. You wouldn't be interested in that.

**You**: Casual sex?

**Society**: Yeah, casual sex. None of the *real* relationships that any discerning person like you or me would want. Just one night stands, tawdry flings, drunken hook-ups that you are only going to regret in the morning. Not like your trusty old normal sexual plane (tap tap)--the choice of the discerning person.

**You**: But "natural" sounds good. I quite like the sound of that. I mean they can't all be short term and tawdry flings.

**Society** (sharp intake of breath): Ooooo, you don't want to choose that one. Oh no!

**You**: But why not?

**Society**: You know who lives over there don't you, *on the natural plane*?

**You**: Who?

**Society**: Only sluts and whores, that's who. Nah, you don't want to be over there.

**You**: Why would that be the case? Why would only sluts and whores like nature?

**Society** (incredulously): Why? Well because there is no enforced monogamy over there on the natural plane. That means they have the choice to love someone freely or to sell themselves.

**You**: And on the normal plane there *is* enforced monogamy? Why would that be better?

**Society**: So that women are *forced* to sell themselves.

**You**: And *how* exactly would that would be better?

**Society**: Well … I mean … I mean women are forced to sell themselves in a *good* way. You know, in exchange for security--the security and happiness of marriage.

**You**: Erm … right.

**Society**: Yes. Good girls do that you see and those good girls, they are all on the normal plane so that's where you want to be (tap tap). So all you need to know is bad girls–natural and good girls – normal (tap tap).

And so society would go on and on, laying on the relationship duress, telling you that unfenced is an illegitimate choice and that you have to choose fenced.

It's true that access to **U**nfenced **L**ong **T**erm **R**elationships (ULTRas) in not an option that most people have. Having access to ULTRas is like the holy grail or lost treasure trove of Sex 3.0, and this fact can be understood only by experiencing it in real life.

If that's what you want, then there is only one thing you need to do--one teeny, tiny, simple little thing. You have to kill the twin-headed monster - jealousy and possessiveness - stone dead!

In the next two chapters, I will tell you how to do that.

# 35 – Why Jealousy Is Not Natural

If you're thinking that unfenced long term relationships (ULTRas) sound like nice in theory, but that jealousy is just a natural emotion that we all have to suffer through in sexual relationships, I have some delightful news for you. It is not.

Jealousy is not, never has been and never will be a natural human emotion.

Jealousy cannot possibly be a natural emotion in human sexual relationships, and here is why.

| Natural /<br>Unfenced | Normal /<br>Fenced |
|---|---|

Remember that in the Sex 2.0 schism, both of these planes operate at the same time, so you can experience things that are normal but at the same time not natural. Like marriage, jealousy is an example of something that is normal but is not natural.

To understand why, we need to define jealousy, and also the difference between jealousy and envy.

Jealousy is exclusively concerned with feelings of insecurity about something you had presumed was your own property.

Envy, on the other hand, can be about anything--your neighbour's perfectly-mowed lawn, your friend's brand new car or girlfriend, or someone else's experience. You could be running for a train, late for a meeting, and be envious of the woman taking her time and enjoying coffee and a freshly-baked pastry while you force yourself to pass the café without stopping.

It's easy to understand the confusion between the two, since people routinely say "I am so jealous" when in fact *they are not jealous, they are envious.* Also, envy and jealousy are closely related, and it's fairly common to experience both at the same time.

To further refine the understanding of jealousy, *sexual* jealousy is exclusively concerned with feelings of insecurity about *a person* who you had presumed was your own sexual property, and now you're not so sure.

Sexual jealousy is that awful sickening sensation--that terrible, sudden feeling of insecurity and dread as you fear that the ground your sexual relationship was built on might be crumbling; the feeling that makes you sick to the stomach. It's the blind anger that comes when somebody else might be trying to take something that is "yours."

If you recognise this feeling, you know jealousy.

Why is it incorrect to regard jealousy as a natural emotion?

Children today, even though we have had the concept of property for many thousands of years, are not born with any concept of property. They are born with no innate or natural concept of ownership.

But it's something that we teach our children from a very young age. For example, preschool children play with "their" toys at home, and then when they go to school they have to learn that toys at school are not "theirs" and have to be shared with other children.

Jealousy can't possibly belong to the natural plane, because the concept of property is not natural, and therefore insecurity over perceived sexual property cannot be natural.

The notion of people as sexual property is something that is a relatively recent artificial human invention and it is *taught* to us.

*We need to unlearn it.*

The normal plane of sexuality, which was introduced at the dawn of Sex 2.0 to deal with the combination of property and paternity concerns, is exactly where jealousy belongs. That's where the twin-headed monster lives, and jealousy belongs there exclusively.

Jealousy cannot possibly operate or function on the natural sexual plane, and cannot have any place whatsoever in unfenced relationships. Unfenced relationships operate exclusively on the natural plane.

Jealousy *is* normal; it is *not*, however, natural.

# 36 – Slaying the Twin Headed Monster

One of the biggest errors you can have on your map is the belief that you *have* to live with the twin-headed monster of jealousy and possessiveness, and that you don't have a choice.

The assumption that the monster is natural and totally unavoidable and nothing can be done about it is a false one.

You don't have to accept that you just have to make a pact with the monster and make peace with it. You don't have to just hope that waiting for the dust to settle after a row and having frenetic make-up sex will do the trick. You don't have to somehow reframe the negative emotions you're feeling as something positive. If that's how you're dealing with jealousy and possessiveness, then you have made a pact with the monster.

You were taught incorrectly your entire life that to have a long term sexual relationship you must have a fenced relationship. Therefore, you have always experienced jealousy in sexual relationships, and may be under the delusion that it is natural. It's not natural; it's only normal.

It's very empowering to know that to rid your life of jealousy forever, you simply have to deselect it.

It's empowering to decide that jealousy and possessiveness are two emotions you don't really enjoy and don't want any more.

I made the point in the "Jealousy and Possessiveness" chapter that if you have jealousy and possessiveness in your life, *you always suffer.*

And I presented you earlier with a very simple choice:

Would you like to suffer, or would you like to not suffer?

If you choose wisely and choose not to suffer, this is what you must do:

KILL THE MONSTER!

Don't make a pact with it, don't reason with it and don't make peace with it.

KILL IT!

Killing the twin-headed monster not only relieves the suffering of jealousy and possessiveness, but it also opens the door to the possibility of loving, pair-bonded, long term *unfenced* relationships (ULTRas), which are not really a viable option in the presence of the twin-headed monster.

If you follow these five steps, you will open the door to that possibility.

## *Step 1 – Realise that killing the monster is possible, and make the choice to do it*

Not only have I done it, but I know many other people who have. If I can do it then so can you. There isn't anything special about me. I did it many years ago, and the effect that it has had on my life has been revolutionary.

I can assure you that it's quite wonderful to not suffer in this way.

My experience of long term, unfenced relationships (which remember does not mean "more than one partner" but simply means no fence and no enforced monogamy), has left me with absolutely zero desire to return to fenced relationships.

Since I have spent half of my adult sex life in each of the camps--fenced and then later unfenced---I feel I have a fairly balanced view of both.

My hope is that you *do* realise it's possible to change, and that you've already made the choice to do it.

Unless those two things are covered, there's no chance of progressing past step 1.

## *Step 2 – Put down the branding iron*

Become familiar with the ideas I've covered, like the difference between jealousy and envy.

Understand that, whilst envy is a natural emotion and fear of loss is also natural, sexual jealousy is not.

Sexual jealousy, which is insecurity over a person you perceive as your sexual property, is uniquely human and is not natural. We are the only species with the notion of property. Since the notion of property itself is an artificial human construct, insecurity over ownership of sexual property is also an artificial construct. It has no place in the natural domain, only the normal domain.

People are not property, so put down the branding iron.

If you think that sexual jealousy is natural because you've observed mate-guarding behaviour in other species--then yes, mate-guarding is natural, but it's simply a form of territoriality about a survival resource. This has nothing to do with property and everything to do with *perceived scarcity*.

What that means is that if you put two bulls in the same field with one cow, they will mate-guard and perhaps even fight to the death over the female. Put the exact same two bulls in a field with 200 cows and they will happily follow their genetic imperative, exhaust themselves by servicing each cow in turn, and won't really feel the need to fight.

Understanding the landscape also means understanding that women and men experience jealousy and possessiveness differently. The differing genetic imperatives guarantee this.

A comprehensive survey of fenced couples was done on this question: [xl]

What would be the worse betrayal: for your partner to have sex with someone else (but not fall in love) or for your partner to fall in love with someone else (but not have sex)?

Men said the worse betrayal would be sex.

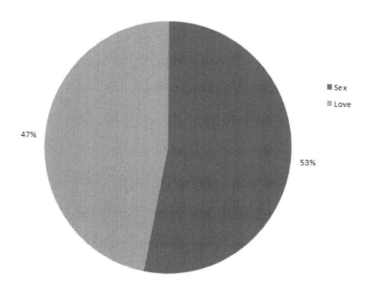

Whereas women said the worse betrayal would be love.

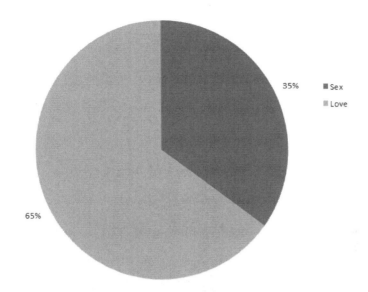

35% ■ Sex
■ Love

65%

In short, the differences are:

Women = I would be afraid that he would fall in love with another woman and leave me

Men = Hey, that's my sexual property!

It's not as black-and-white as that (as reflected in the percentages), but you can see the clear differences between the sexes, and if you understand the differing genetic imperatives, it's easy to understand why those differences exist.

## Step 3 – Accept envy

Unlike sexual jealousy, envy is a natural emotion. Don't fight it. Just accept it.

Envy is really just a feeling of discontent with the perceived advantage or position of another person. Unlike jealousy, it's not really avoidable.

After all, there are only 24 hours in a day. Let's say you're in an unfenced relationship and you wish to spend a particular evening with a partner but can't because they're with another partner of theirs who doesn't wish to share for the evening. You might then feel envious, even if you've already slain the twin-headed monster.

It's not a pleasant emotion to experience, but compared to the potent mixture of rage and sick-to-your-stomach insecurity that jealousy can be, it's a piece of cake. Trust me.

Dealing with envy is really just as simple as accepting that you will see that partner another time.

And in a long term unfenced relationship, even envy dissipates over time like dust in the wind.

## Step 4 – Intellectual acceptance

Know and accept that jealousy and possessiveness have absolutely no place whatsoever in unfenced relationships

Know and accept that, if you are in an unfenced relationship, you cannot engage in policing behaviour.

That means do not ask or answer jealous or possessive questions about where you were or who you might have been with. Do not become an amateur sleuth and check others' text messages or emails.

Understand that if you think loving someone makes policing behaviour OK, then you are doing nothing more than welcoming the twin-headed monster into your relationship. If that's where you are emotionally, then you're fenced, regardless of whether you have a verbal agreement with your partner to be unfenced.

Be conscious enough about your own behaviour to catch yourself when you engage in policing behaviour or feel even the slightest desire to do so.

You cannot police and patrol a fence that *does not exist*. That's insane; realise it.

If your partner in an unfenced relationship does any of those things, then make it clear that they're trying to police a fence that doesn't exist and they need to stop.

If your partner is aware that they're in an unfenced relationship and they persist in such behaviour even after you make this clear, then the relationship has no future. You are trying to mix oil and water at this point, and they don't mix.

In unfenced relationships, permission is not required for you to exercise your option, nor for your partner to exercise theirs. Accept that.

If only one partner is choosing to exercise their option, or one partner is exercising their option more frequently than the other, that's fine. Accept it.

In unfenced relationships it's not possible to cheat. Cheating involves establishing a fence and then hopping over it while your partner isn't looking. There's no fence to hop over here. Accept it.

## Step 5 – Emotional acceptance

If you have spent your entire life trying to follow the standard script and have never even attempted a long term unfenced relationship, then the emotional acceptance step will be more challenging than the intellectual acceptance step.

Emotionally, an unfenced relationship will just go against the grain and against the landscape of what you're used to. Well-established emotional patterns need to be unlearned.

The good news is that, once you have unlearned them, you never have to do it again. In other words, you don't have to go through this five-step process again if or when you start a new relationship.

The first time you attempt an unfenced pair-bonded relationship, what happens initially when you find out you're your partner is with somebody else is the kneejerk response of jealousy and possessiveness. It feels awful.

That's what you've been used to your entire life, so the conditioned response will come out at first. The same unbearable sense of insecurity will surface automatically and the feelings of being in an unfamiliar emotional landscape will hit you, as will the reality that you accepted this and consented to it.

Jealousy will feel natural, even though it isn't. It was chosen for you and you must learn to deselect it.

Essentially at this stage you are emotionally dealing with the root cause of possessiveness too. Whilst the root cause of sexual jealousy is insecurity over what you perceive as your sexual property, the root cause of possessiveness is fear of loss.

These are closely connected feelings, and in unfenced relationships they are dealt with at an emotional level in the same way:

--By emotionally accepting that you will be together as long as you both wish to be together.

--By realising that there's nothing more loving than both people choosing to return to each other time and time again when offered free choice.

--By knowing you are returning to each other because you want to, and not because you have a sole-sex-provider agreement by which not returning to them means the choice of either sexually starving or breaking up.

--By realising that one cannot possibly fear losing all access to sex if there is no fence and you always have the option of other partners (whether you choose to use the option or not). Fear of loss can exist only with a scarcity mentality. Rid yourself of this mentality.

The fear of loss quickly subsides in both you and your partner as your return to each other over and over again. The desire to return is actively reinforced by the fact that you never argue over jealousy and possessive bullshit and you know you can be honest with each other.

Two of the primary reasons people break up are arguing over jealousy/possessiveness, or because they want their sexual freedom back (i.e. their freedom to see other people). Unfencing removes both reasons.

People in unfenced relationships essentially don't have many reasons to break up. It's very unusual in such relationships for love to die, except for reasons related to the four pillars of pure form relationships – communication, honesty, trust and respect.

*Love never dies a natural death. It dies because we don't know how to replenish its source. It dies of blindness and errors and betrayals. It dies of illness and wounds; it dies of weariness, of withering, of tarnishing – Anais Nin*

Once you've slain the twin-headed monster you should never have to do it again. Once dead, he stays dead as long as you stick to these principles and don't allow yourself to regress into bad habits.

When you've removed the primary source of poison in sexual relationships, you're never again going to enter step four (the spin cycle) of the twin-headed monster sequence in relationships.

When you get to this point--congratulations! You've killed the twin-headed monster, and made it to the other side.

# 37 – The Death of the Pacman, the Slut and the Whore

These three characters go out the window in a Sex 3.0 world. Let's take them one by one to find out why.

## The Pacman

Yes, he is dead (cue Pacman death sound effect).

PAC (paternity concern) was dealt with in the Sex 2.0 era by the invention of marriage and the selling of the Sex 2.0 deal. Women were told they had to sell their sexuality to a man in exchange for security, and men were told they had to make women their sexual property. The whole thing was enforced by a barrage of relationship duress, just to be extra sure.

But as we've said, this whole construct did not even guarantee paternity. What is politely termed "paternity discrepancy" in modern society is conservatively estimated to run to about 20 percent.

That's a fairly high failure rate for a system designed entirely to guard against such failures. DNA paternity testing, on the other hand, has a success rate of greater than 99.9% [xli]

In short, if you want to guarantee that you're not being cuckolded into raising somebody else's child, being a PACman is a bad way to go about it. Sex 3.0 recognises this, and there are no PACmen in a Sex 3.0 world.

## The Slut

As there are no PACmen, there are also no sluts.

To re-cap: men and women call women sluts for different reasons.

When a man calls a woman a slut, he's saying either that she's advertising her sexuality in a way that triggers his PAC, or she's having more sex than he approves of and it triggers his PAC. So, as far as the male side of the equation goes, no Pacmen means no sluts.

When a woman calls a woman a slut it means she's accusing her of breaking the Sex 2.0 deal that says women have to sell their sexuality in exchange for security. She's saying, "You're giving away something for free that I believe *I* need to sell in order to survive!"

Women essentially "police" other women by shaming them in this manner because they believe they need to do so to ensure that the Sex 2.0 deal remains viable. Women who don't follow the agenda are breaking "union rules" and are traitors to their own gender.

But the Sex 2.0 deal is dead. No Sex 2.0 deal means there are no sluts.

## The Whore

There are no whores in a Sex 3.0 world either, but by that I don't mean there are no women having sex in exchange for cash.

Whether prostitution is "the world's oldest profession" is debatable (it seems to me that farming came first), but one thing we can be sure of is that it's not going away any time soon, and certainly not in the Sex 3.0 era.

So there will be prostitutes in a Sex 3.0 world but no whores, because "whore," like "slut," is simply a shaming word used for women who threatened the Sex 2.0 deal by not following it.

With no Sex 2.0 deal to be threatened, there are no shaming words for people who threaten it. The idea that consensual sex between adults is somehow wrong is a very, very Sex 2.0 concept that has no place in a Sex 3.0 world.

Sure, if one or both parties are in a fenced relationship, then that is dishonest and dishonesty is not a good thing. However, it's the dishonest component that's wrong, not the consensual sex component.

Unless it's done dishonestly or between close relatives, it's hard to see any circumstance in which consenting adults having sex together is wrong.


## Cruel Choice Committee Disbanded

Notice to cruel choice committee members: you have been disbanded.

With the death of the Sex 2.0 deal, and along with it the Pacman, the slut and the whore, it's clear that this committee has no reason to continue.

That means women will no longer be presented with the cruel choice of either selling their sexuality in exchange for security in relationships based on sexual ownership, or else being labelled a slut or a whore.

Women no longer need to play a leading role in the suppression of their own sexuality or their own gender, nor do they need to call each other sluts or whores. As the Sex 2.0 deal is dead, there's no point any more.

Women no longer need to be judged by both men and women their entire lives for engaging in a basic human need. Nor do they need to pretend that they don't like sex, try to delay or avoid it lest they are thought of as "too easy," nor concern themselves with having a low number of bedpost notches in order to have a good reputation.

In Sex 3.0 we – both men and women - get to stop shaming women in order to control their sexuality. Ultimately everybody has suffered because of it.

Unmarried women who want to have sex do not need to seek shelter under the safe umbrella of boyfriend/girlfriend relationships in order to avoid the barbs and arrows directed at those who don't.

Boyfriend/girlfriend relationships now become a choice in the true sense of the word, and not just a safe shelter from societal shaming.

Men benefit too. Since men and women are not monogamous by nature, they no longer need to be forced by society into duplicity (one that's relatively easy to maintain in the early infatuation stage of a relationship, but not for life).

Duplicity disappears in Sex 3.0, and both cards are on the table in plain view.

| Natural /<br>Unfenced | | Normal /<br>Fenced |
|---|---|---|

Also on the table in plain view are the historic reasons for why there are two planes of human sexuality in the first place.

All this needs to be well understood in Sex 3.0, in order to give us a map that better reflects the territory. We need to know how and why we got here.

## Backwards-compatible

Since you have the free, open and honest choice of fenced or unfenced in a Sex 3.0 world, Sex 3.0 is nicely backwards-compatible with Sex 2.0. You can still have a conventional boyfriend/girlfriend relationship in a Sex 3.0 world, and you can still have a conventional marriage too. (I told you that you could bring those handcuffs along and use them here too if you wanted to--didn't I, you kinky thing?)

The fact that these conventional options are more of an honest and informed choice is a huge improvement.

Sex 3.0 lays the cards on the table, points out the relative merits of fenced and unfenced, and under no duress whatsoever says, "Hey, it's your life so you choose."

Sex 2.0 = Unfenced is hidden. Fenced is promoted under duress.

Sex 3.0 = Nothing is hidden. Make your choice. No duress.

# 38 – The Death of Relationship Duress

Ding dong, the witch is dead! Which old witch? The wicked witch!

Relationship duress was invented at the beginning of the Sex 2.0 era to enforce the Sex 2.0 deal. Guess what? The death of that deal means not only that relationship duress is no longer necessary, but that it's a completely bankrupt concept.

Relationship duress has no place whatsoever in a Sex 3.0 world

Not only does that relieve us of the self-replicating nature of the mapping errors that I discussed at the beginning of the book, but it relieves us of the whole societally-sanctioned fenced relationship agenda and all the RD nonsense that goes along with it.

What follows is a list of such RD nonsense, which in Sex 3.0 we are thankfully rid of. (This is not an exhaustive list, because that would make this book the size of an encyclopaedia.)

## Promotion of "the one"

The most ridiculous Sex 2.0 myth of all is the myth of "the one."

There are about 7,000,000,000 people in the world right now. Half of them match your sexual preference (or maybe all of them if you are bi), which is 3,500,000,000 people. Take away the ones that are too old or young or infirm, and that still leaves more than 1,000,000,000 people.

Let's say you're exceptionally picky and would find only 5% of those remaining people attractive. You are still left with 50,000,000 people.

Let's make a conservative and pessimistic estimate and say that amazing chemistry and fireworks could happen with only 5% of the attractive people. That's 2,500,000 people.

You see the problem with the idea of "the one?"

Take a large country with a large population like the USA, which has only three cities with a population greater than 2,500,000: NY, LA and Chicago.

2,500,000 is very close to the population of Chicago. Imagine living in such a city, except that every single person there matches not only your gender preference but your physical type as well, and has the amazing chemistry and fireworks that would happen if you got to know each other.

Do you still believe in the one?

I'm not saying there isn't a very, very special person out there for everyone. I believe there is. But I'm saying that if for one reason or another it doesn't work out with that person, there are plenty of fish left in the sea. This is a good thing.

One can't maintain a belief in "the one" and a belief that there are "plenty of fish in the sea" at the same time. They're mutually exclusive concepts.

You probably know which one is really true, and that the notion of "the one" was simply used by society to promote the fenced agenda.

## The lonely spinster/bachelor myth

This one says that if you don't marry you're going to die alone and sad.

This is not only complete nonsense; it's the opposite of the truth.

Picture yourself living your entire adult life, approximately 60 years, engaging in loving, long term unfenced relationships. To do so, you must already have killed the twin-headed monster, which means there's no real reason to break up with people (unless a relationship violates one or more of the four pure-form pillars).

By the time you reach the end of your days you will have many long term loving relationships. Of course you won't die alone.

Farming out all of your sexual needs to one person on an exclusive basis, on the other hand, drastically increases your chances of dying alone. If you have only one partner and they pull the plug on the relationship or die before you do, you've lost 100% of your loving and sexually-intimate relationships.

If that happens during a lifetime of long term unfenced relationships, you've lost only a fraction of your loving and sexually-intimate relationships

## The idea that not to see people as they really are is a good thing

Romance is just romance. Romantic love/infatuation emotions fade after a while because they're supposed to. You just come to see the person as they really are and not as some idealised vision of perfection.

This is not because you have "lost the magic that you had at the beginning" or because maybe this is not "the one." It's because nature intends it to be this way. You are not meant to be with one person on an exclusive basis for life.

The idea that a romantic fairy tale is a desirable replacement for reality is an odd one anyway. Since when is making long term plans based on short term emotions a good thing?

*The idea that relationships are supposed to be "hard work" and that if you "work on your relationship" it's a sign of maturity*

Relationships are no more than mutual reward. They are supposed to be simple and not complicated. They are supposed to be completely self-sustaining and they are not supposed to be hard work. You are not "supposed" to argue and then work things out afterwards. This is not a sign of maturity.

The idea that relationships are supposed to be hard work is just a backwards rationalisation to excuse the presence of difficulties which have been introduced completely and totally unnecessarily. It's a way of sugar-coating a bitter pill that people believe they have to swallow when they don't.

Inviting the twin-header monster in is now a choice, and you know that now. Stagnation by exclusivity is a choice. You have choices in Sex 3.0.

If you don't want the twin-header monster in your life, then kill him!

If you don't want stagnation by exclusivity, then don't be exclusive.

You don't have to do much, if any, work at all to maintain your relationships with your best friends, do you? If you think, "oh well that's different," of course it's different--but only because we've made it so.

## The promotion of the idea of marriage as traditional

Anybody who watched live coverage of the royal wedding of Prince William and Kate Middleton would have lost count of the amount of times the commentators used the word "traditional." It felt like one out of every three words was about tradition--above all, the wonderful tradition of marriage.

Marriage *is* traditional. But there's one thing even more traditional than getting married, and that's *not* getting married.

In the last approximately 200,000 years, human beings (and our immediate ancestors) started getting married only about 10,000 years ago, which means marriage is something we *have* done for about 5% of the time (the most recent 5% at that) and something we have *not* done for about 95% of the time.

This means that non-marriage is approximately 1,900% more traditional than marriage, and that's a conservative estimate when you bear in mind that far fewer than 100% of people get married. Also, you have to remember how long it took for the agricultural revolution (and with it the concept of marriage) to spread globally. So a more accurate figure would indicate that non-marriage is about 5,000% more traditional than marriage, but you get the point.

In Sex 3.0 we get to stop using words like "traditional" and "old fashioned" to describe things human beings have begun to do so relatively recently.

## The idea that marriage is romantic

Romance means placing an idealised value on something that is far beyond its actual value. You can romanticise people, including sexual partners, or inanimate objects like family heirlooms. You can even romanticise something that doesn't even physically exist, like a period of time. People constantly romanticise London in the swinging sixties and Paris in the 1930s.

Marriage is not romantic – to paraphrase a famous quote, romance is a temporary insanity best cured by marriage – but wedding ceremonies certainly *are* romantic. The more ridiculously lavish they are, the more romantic.

*"All marriages are happy. It's the living together afterwards that causes all the trouble." – Raymond Hull*

The actual marriage itself cannot be romantic, not only because you get used to each other and see each other as you really are afterwards, but also because there's nothing romantic at all about the notion of rightful sexual property.

## The fuck buddy fallacy

Unfenced relationships--just like fenced relationships--can be loving and pair-bonded, or not.

The fuck buddy fallacy says that, unless the relationship is fenced, it's just casual sex, you're merely friends with benefits or fuck buddies, and it's not a "real" relationship.

It's a very, very Sex 2.0 idea to assume that, because your relationships aren't based on sexual ownership, sex is the only aspect of the relationships.

The idea that a relationship must be fenced in order to be meaningful is silly. Any truly loving and pair-bonded relationship is meaningful, regardless of whether it's fenced or not.

## Self-flagellation

To put it mildly, the design of Sex 2.0 is a joke. Not only is it a joke, it's a joke in very poor taste.

The amount of failures that are systemic to the very core of its design is alarming.

Because RD overwhelmingly tells people that Sex 2.0 and fenced relationships are the *only* way to conduct their love lives, the failure of a relationship makes people think the problem is with them. Fenced relationships *can't* be wrong! The idea of fencing itself *can't* be to blame!

Although someone might be tempted to blame the failure of any one relationship on their ex-partner, not on themselves or their map, a decade or so of failed relationships can cause people to really beat themselves up emotionally. Repeated failures feel like a personal failure, and can cause low self-esteem, massive depression, and the tendency to medicate emotions with drugs and alcohol.

I say the Sex 2.0 design is a joke in poor taste because it costs human *lives* on a daily basis, either through suicide caused by such depression, or murder caused by jealousy and possessiveness.

No more.


## The bad doctor and his bad medicine

Society is like a doctor. Doctors prescribe medicines, society prescribes beliefs.

Society is not always a good doctor though. Sometimes it gives you medicine that makes you sick, like the idea that you must base your relationships on the concept of sexual ownership.

RD insists that you swallow that medicine. With no RD in Sex 3.0, you don't have to take the bad medicine any more.

## The "Big No" agenda

Religion sells the idea that sex is sinful, not honourable. It preaches about immorality and "bad girls," and teaches people to feel guilty about sex. I call this the "Big No" agenda.

This is clearly RD, and it has no place in Sex 3.0. Sex is natural and exists to be enjoyed.

## The "other half" myth

The idea that you need "another half" to complete you is not only obvious RD, but it's responsible for a lot of unhappiness because people don't give themselves permission to be happy as they are.

People who are taught this believe that the source of their happiness is external and that they're incomplete and cannot possibly be happy simply from within.

In Sex 3.0 we're thankfully rid of this dangerous notion.

## Pressure from immediate family and close friends to settle down

In the Sex 2.0 world, this is the root cause of an awful lot of arguments with those you are close to.

Living in a Sex 3.0 world, you begin to see things like RD in the proper perspective. Whereas in the past you might have gotten upset and argued, you're now more likely to simply observe it and think, "Hmm. Sex 2.0 RD. Interesting."

## The Madonna/Whore Syndrome

Men who suffer from this are by and large Pacmen. Central to the mentality of the Pacman is the notion that "good girls don't," so they have a polarised view of women as either saints who ideally don't even like sex and should be revered, or as whores who are to be despised for their wantonness. [xlii]

Women in the Sex 2.0 marketplace know that many men think like this, and in order to maintain their market value, they respond with a "pussy probation period." In other words they think, "If I make him wait, he'll respect me and if I don't then he won't."

This rather bizarre quirk of the Sex 2.0 marketplace means that quite often a woman will date a guy, be really attracted to him, want to have sex with him, but won't have sex with him precisely because she likes him so much.

She might tell herself, "I don't want to just have sex with him, I want to date him."

She might not have a problem at all with the idea of picking up a random guy in a bar and banging him later the very same night on the down-low because "that doesn't count." She's afraid that if she doesn't make the guy she really likes wait for a while, she might never see him again because he regards her as "too easy."

If you think that's bizarre, what about the guy with the Madonna/whore syndrome who regards women who ideally don't even like sex as a good girls and "marriage material?"

Does being married to a woman with no noticeable appetite for sex sound like a recipe for a healthy married sex life?

Since this is all RD caused mostly by Pacmen, we now give ourselves permission to throw such silly attitudes out the window.

## The idea that female virginity is a prized asset

This is a very damaging, unhealthy and completely ridiculous notion from the Sex 2.0 world.

We've already covered the historical reasons for this notion. A man in the Sex 2.0 world thinks his best chance of ensuring lines of heritage and of not being cuckolded is to fence in a virgin female and to mate-guard her at least until she provides him with a first born.

However, sex is healthy. When you have sex your body is flooded with all kinds of reward-giving hormones and chemicals that make you feel great. Not having sex is not healthy.

Any woman who believes in this notion is not only punishing herself by living an unhealthily sexless lifestyle as a result, but is considering herself an asset to be sold.

In other words, she is asserting to herself that her pussy is property, and punishing herself with a sexless existence in order to maintain what she falsely perceives as its high sale value in the sexual marketplace.

To say this is a backward notion is an understatement, and it's one that's damaging for both men and women. I remember when I was travelling on this research trip through Turkey--a country with an extraordinarily high level of RD in my experience. I was speaking with a local guy about this subject and he said "you wouldn't want to buy a car that had miles on the clock, would you?" to which I replied, "You wouldn't want to hire a chauffeur who'd never driven a car, would you?"

Imagine the ad: "Chauffer required. Must have no driving licence and no prior experience of driving a car or any other kind of vehicle.

Preference will be given to those who have never even been inside a car."

### The idea that anyone who enjoys sex outside of marriage is attacking marriage

This is pure RD nonsense. It's like saying that someone who enjoys walking to work is attacking public transportation.

*The insistence on false advertising*

I'm not just talking about the dishonest manner in which the choice of unfenced relationships is hidden. RD insists that we falsely advertise all kind of things about sexuality to each other constantly, like the myth of monogamy as natural and the idea of the female as demure and reluctant when it comes to sexual enjoyment.

This is a charade that women engage in to avoid (at best) being on the receiving end of shaming language from both men and women, and (at worst) being shunned by her family or village, or stoned to death.

As someone who routinely offers women non-judgemental acceptance of their sexual nature, I've seen countless times the look of relief on a woman's face when she realises that it's safe in my company for her to "come out of hiding" and stop pretending she's not so sexual.

Who enjoys sex more--men or women? If anyone reading this has doubts about women's level of sexual enjoyment, and is looking for proof, I suggest that the next time you're having sex, you … oh I don't know … maybe just open you ears and really listen to the noises women make.

Or if you're not in a sexual relationship, then check into the nearest love motel and hold a glass to the wall. Come to think of it, forget the glass—you're not going to need it.

"Yeeeeeesssss! Oh yesssssss! AGHHHH! Yeah, that's it! Right there!! OH MY GOD! OH MY GOD! OH MY GOD! ooOOOOOooOOOOo! Oooohhh baby! Fuck me like that! Yeah! Fuck me! Pull my hair! Yeahhhhh! Spank me! SPANK ME! That's right!! I'm your little whore! Arrrrrrrrrrrr! OH MY GOD! OH MY GOD! OH MY GOD!! "

As for guys? We mostly just grunt and comply with spanking, hair-pulling and name-calling requests.

Case closed.

## Removing the fenced-tinted glasses

When society observes that rare thing in a Sex 2.0 world--a couple in an unfenced relationship who are brave enough not to hide it, and then that relationship breaks down, then it's taken as definitive proof that "open relationships" fundamentally just don't work.

However, oddly enough, when a conventional fenced relationship breaks down, that's not taken as any sign at all that fenced relationships don't work. This is an obvious double standard and a blatant piece of RD. Time to get rid of it.

## Dogma

The death of relationship duress means the death of dogma in the sexual realm and the end of living your entire lives, when it comes to sexual relationships, in the shadow of the thoughts, beliefs and coercion of other people. [xliii]

Sex 2.0 = dogmatic

Sex 3.0 = not dogmatic

Only without dogma can you be truly free.

*"Your time is limited; don't waste it living someone else's life."*
*--Steve Jobs*

The idea that it's acceptable to tell other people to live *their* sex lives by *your* value system is rather repulsive, but it's accepted in a Sex 2.0 society. Not in Sex 3.0.

The foregoing is not an exhaustive list of Sex 2.0 RD, but like I said, I didn't want to write an encyclopaedia.

So—yes, the wicked witch is dead! She is truly and finally dead.

We really should celebrate, because relationship duress has always been anti-human, inauthentic and pathological, as well as against the definition of the word relationship.

Leaving behind RD also means…

# 39 – Un-Screwing Gays and Lesbians the Sex 3.0 Way

Earlier I pointed out how Sex 2.0 totally screws gay men and lesbians but not in a way that they like being screwed. How does this change in the Sex 3.0 world?

The normal plane still exists in Sex 3.0, but anybody who's aware understands the difference between the normal and the natural sexual planes perfectly well, and would never be so dim-witted as to falsely accuse gays or lesbians of being un-natural.

This alone represents at least some kind of progress.

The more Sex 3.0 people there are in the world, the greater will be the acceptance of same-sex attraction as natural. The more the acceptance of gays and lesbians grows, the less intolerance there will be, and the more normalisation of homosexuality.

Particularly in large cities in the western world, the gay and lesbian community is becoming more accepted, thanks to a mixture of activism, high-profile gay and lesbian celebrities, media coverage, and more roles for gay and lesbian characters in mainstream entertainment. A culture is being created where people feel more comfortable coming out of the closet, or never being in the closet in the first place.

Gay people might also be helped if society's conservative elements have a new enemy. Bearing in mind that many conservative moralists are now far more hesitant to decry either gays and lesbians for fear of being called homophobic (a label just as likely to be wielded by straights as by gay people these days), then yes--conservatives do need a new enemy. Well, they've got one.

Unfenced is the new gay, or at least it has a chance of being. I'm pretty sure conservative elements in society will get themselves into a froth about it (I can't bring myself to call them defenders of "traditional" morals, since being unfenced is, as I pointed out earlier, about 5,000% more traditional than being fenced, so the high ground of tradition belongs to the unfenced if it belongs to anyone).

Anyway, if they do get themselves into a tizzy, they're just showing themselves to be the nature-phobes that they are.

Since heterosexual, gay and lesbian people can all be in unfenced relationships with the gender they prefer, we can all fight side-by-side for the right to not be discriminated against or shamed for being unfenced.

All together now:

"One, two, three, four--fences really are a bore! Five, six, seven, eight--fenced is what we really hate!"

# 40 – Belonging in a Sex 3.0 World

Now that we've taken a look at some of the principles of Sex 3.0, it's time to look at the Sex 3.0 marketplace and how it operates.

## A Quick History of Belonging

People in a Sex 3.0 world "belong" in a fundamentally different way than how they belonged previously.

Let's review:

- Sex 1.0 = voluntary belonging (unfenced).

- Sex 2.0 = mandated belonging based on sexual ownership (fenced), under duress from society.

- Sex 3.0 = the choice of either fenced or unfenced. No duress whatsoever.

It's not a coincidence that slavery was invented during the Sex 2.0 era of human history. When human beings had no concept of property, money or an economy (Sex 1.0), there could also be no concept of slavery.

After property was invented, coming up with the idea of *people* as property was not a big leap. And slavery has been present in pretty much every Sex 2.0-era civilization ever studied and recorded: ancient India, Greece, China, Egypt, the Roman Empire, the Americas and so on. [xliv]

It's only in very, very recent human history--as recently as 1948--that the U.N. declared freedom from slavery as an internationally-recognised human right. [xlv]

So we've had 10,000 years of slavery and only 50 years of non-slavery, and even those 50 years are questionable, since human trafficking still goes on today.

There have always been different forms of slavery, including forced labour, bonded labour, human trafficking and so on. But from a slaves' point of view, slavery is just when you do what you're told to in order to stay alive and to not be punished.

Before effective contraception and the welfare state, unmarried women put themselves at tremendous risk if they had sex with a man. To do so without risking death or punishment meant they had to comply with the Sex 2.0 deal and sexually belong to a husband. In that light, Sex 2.0 can be seen as a form of slavery.

Hypergamy (finding the best provider to whom they could sell their sexuality) became a woman's best survival strategy during this era. Having that choice was the main thing that differentiated them from slaves who had no choice about their master. Often women didn't have even that choice, because the family made the choice for them. [xlvi]

Marrying for love is only a very recent phenomenon historically. It's a luxury afforded only in certain cultures and at certain points in their history when marriage became a choice and was not necessary for survival. [xlvii]

In modern Western society the idea of slave ownership is preposterous. The very mention of it would make people look at you like you were crazy.

So even though it's been in existence for almost the entire Sex 2.0 era, slavery is a concept that we human beings have deeply scrutinised. And our conclusion is that slavery is really not very human of us at all. Mainstream international society has shaken off slavery and abandoned it as inhumane.

So, the quick human history of belonging goes like this:

    1 - Property invented

    2 - People become property both as slave labour (men and women) and as sexual property (women)

    3 - The concept of people as slave labour is internationally abandoned

    4 - The concept of women as sexual property is internationally abandoned

We have done the first three, but so far not the fourth. We have yet to leave behind the notion of women as sexual property, even though with the death of the Sex 2.0 deal there are no remaining reasons not to do so.

The thing about belonging is that people don't really enjoy being owned. They don't enjoy being stamped, labelled or branded as property, neither men nor women. Whilst that treatment does provide a certain type of belonging and security, it's not a kind of belonging that people enjoy very much.

A voluntary and loving sense of belonging, on the other hand, is deeply satisfying. However, the only way to get a voluntary sense of belonging in the Sex 2.0 world is by having a serially-monogamous dating life, or by marrying and not taking your "till death do us part" vow literally but rather holding it as an ideal and leaving if the relationship doesn't work out.

Either way, Sex 2.0 forces people into duplicity, because marriage is meant to be for life and dating is meant to lead to marriage. Dating is not supposed to be a way for girls to have pair-bonded sexy time and escape the RD label of slut, nor for guys to use as a way of marking a girl they're having sex with as "off limits" to other guys which is mostly what it is currently used for.

This dynamic changes in the Sex 3.0 marketplace.

# 41 – Fenced or Unfenced?

The best way to offer a true sense of belonging is to abolish relationship duress from the marketplace completely and to make the process as totally transparent and honest as possible. That's exactly what happens in the Sex 3.0 marketplace.

Everything is a choice. Nothing is an obligation.

Everything is clear. Nothing is hidden.

Your choice is as clear as this:

|  |  |
|---|---|
| Natural /<br>Unfenced | Normal /<br>Fenced |

One of the misconceptions that may arise around the issues that I discuss in this book is the notion that I'm against fenced relationships. After all, I've spent a significant amount of time explaining the obstacles that fenced couples, sometimes unwittingly, throw in their own path.

I have nothing against fenced relationships at all. I am, however, very much against self-deception or any other kind of deception for that matter.

Society should not lie about your choices, nor should it use relationship duress to dogmatically strong-arm the world's population into living a life in which they feel that they don't have a choice, or that long term sexual relationships are valid only if fenced.

Anything positive that can possibly flower in a fenced relationship can also flower in an unfenced relationship. And all relationships that are loving and pair-bonded are valid, whether fenced or not.

How strong any relationship stays does not depend on whether it's fenced or unfenced. It depends on love, on the quality of the pair-bond, and on whether both parties do their utmost to maintain the four pillars of communication, honesty, trust and respect.

## Which is better?

The debate about whether fenced or unfenced is better is a totally pointless one and a complete waste of time.

In fact, I would go so far as to say that anybody wishing to enter into such a debate is seeking to prove that their choice is better and that those who make a different choice are wrong or stupid. See the problem with that? Yes—it's simply another example of relationship duress.

If you consider yourself a Sex 3.0 kind of person and find yourself getting involved in this debate, then just stop and realise what you're doing. Only Sex 2.0 people involve themselves in matters of relationship duress.

You may well find yourself on the receiving end of Sex 2.0 RD if or when people find out you're in an unfenced relationship. If that situation happens, just realise that they're projecting their fears about the accuracy of their own map onto you. Just smile and remind yourself that they're parroting Sex 2.0 programming.

People will insist that you act the way they and other people act, and that if you don't you're weird and very wrong.

Do not seek to prove yourself right and them wrong. That's a fool's game, and like all fool's games, the only winning move is to not play.

The only question that really matters regarding fenced or unfenced is which one is right for you.

The only person who can hold that debate and make that decision is you.

## How to Choose

Hopefully reading this far has given you a good idea of the sexual landscape past and present.

As I've pointed out, Sex 3.0 is backwards-compatible, meaning you can still have a conventional monogamous boyfriend/girlfriend relationship or a conventional marriage, but the differences are that:

> • You make the choice in full knowledge of the obstacles that may crop up along the way. This alone is a better way of going about things because your chances of swerving or successfully dealing with the obstacles are increased when you know they're there. The knowledge gives you a better map.

> • You make the choice fully aware that you have the alternate choice of unfenced relationships. Under Sex 2.0 most people enter fenced relationships blindly because they don't realise they have a choice. They're under the mistaken impression that if they don't enter into a fenced relationship with the person they hooked

up with, it becomes fenced by default if they keep seeing each other so their only other choices are to one-night-stand the guy or pump-and-dump the girl.

• You are taking responsibility for your choices. As I pointed out earlier in the book, many people don't blame their map or the bad doctor when things go wrong, they blame their partner and that's why their map never gets fixed. If you chose fenced and you experience jealous / possessive problems in the relationship then you should take responsibility for your choice of fenced.

• You are making a choice in the complete absence of relationship duress. Relationship duress is a bankrupt concept.

I spent the first half of my adult sex life (a little more than a decade) on the normal plane in fenced relationships (or at least trying to be), and the second half of my adult sex life on the natural plane in unfenced relationships. I feel I have a good view of both worlds, and I've given the subject as much objective clarity as I possibly can.

If you enjoy taking security from the promised sexual exclusivity of your relationships, even though it's not guaranteed; if you accept that cheating can be devastating but you're confident that that won't happen and you won't be tempted to stray either; and if you're confident about dealing with the dangers of jealousy and possessiveness as well as the dangers of stagnation by exclusivity and familiarity--then it sounds like fenced is for you.

If you want to get married, then obviously fenced is for you. By its nature, marriage is fenced.

## 42 – Marriage in the Sex 3.0 Marketplace

Another possible misconception that may arise from reading this book is that I'm trying to weaken or undermine marriage. This is the opposite of the truth.

I also am not suggesting that a higher percentage of people *should* get married. Remember that any time someone says "you should" or "you must" when it comes to how *you* run *your* relationships, they're practicing a form of relationship duress.

Sex 3.0 marriage can never happen as a result of relationship duress because RD does not exist in Sex 3.0. Contrast two couples:

Couple one forms a marriage after being presented with the choice of fenced or unfenced. They're fully aware of the relative merits of the two choices, and together both choose marriage--not because they think they have to or it's expected of them by society. They make that choice under no duress, are aware of the obstacles ahead, and are aware of the historical reasons why marriage was invented.

Couple two gets married under duress from society and their family, without knowledge about fenced and unfenced, and because marriage is expected even though they probably don't even know why it was invented.

Couple one will almost certainly be entering marriage because they love each other and think that a *legally* fenced relationship is best for them and their children.

Couple two on the other hand may well be entering marriage with a mix of love and fear (or perhaps no love at all if it's an arranged marriage), and are doing so because it's expected.

Couple one had a choice. Couple two had an obligation enforced by dogma and duress.

Couple one was aware of both the choice that they made (fenced as opposed to unfenced), and the obstacles ahead of them. Couple two was not.

Which marriage do you think is likelier to succeed?

## The Future of Marriage

I started to write about marriage and parenthood extensively in an early draft of this book, but it took up so many words that I realised it belongs in a separate book (one I may well write in the future).

But let's look briefly here at the future of marriage. The evolution of the institution, if it's to remain relevant and viable to society at large, must inevitably follow a course that's more in tune with nature. It cannot require people to take oaths that are so difficult to keep because they don't respect human nature.

The rapidly declining numbers of people getting married worldwide (Germany, the UK, France, the USA, etc) indicate that for many the notions of eternal marriage and a lifetime of monogamy are unrealistic and obsolete. How could we not conclude that when surrounded by evidence of systemic marital failure?

France is an interesting case study. Back in 1999 the French created a system of civil unions called pacte civil de solidarité

(PACS), which at the time was heralded as breakthrough legislation for gay and lesbian couples wishing to "tie the knot." [xlviii]

PACS isn't quite like marriage, in that it can be dissolved with a simple registered letter, but it has many of the same legal advantages--like medical benefits and tax breaks.

The legislation was worded in such a way, however, that it wasn't restricted to gay and lesbian couples. The result was that in 2000--the year after the legislation was passed--75% of PACS were between heterosexual couples. In recent years that number has risen to 95%.

This is the rise of the new family--one that says let love bloom and run its natural course, however long that may be, and let everyone accept that it works until it doesn't work. In other words, PACS are aligned with the true meaning of the word relationship; the relationship exists as long as mutual reward exists.

If you think that marriage is more workable or higher functioning than PACS, consider this: A report on identical-length unions of both kinds showed that one in ten PACS are dissolved, compared to one out of every three marriages.[xlix]

If you think that more relationship duress, as in high-RD countries in the Middle East, is the solution for making make marriages higher-functioning, consider this:

The divorce rate in Saudi Arabia in 2011 was approximately 62%, which is even higher than in Western countries, where it typically hovers around 50%.[l]

As for alternatives to marriage, there are more options than just civil unions. Commitment ceremonies and other forms of non-marriage-based unions are becoming more popular, whilst marriage is declining. People are questioning the legitimacy of marriage and the notion that you need a state-issued license in order to have commitment, love or a family.

The way groupthink work dictates that there are still many who think marriage is morally right, and that a decline in marriages equates to a decline in the morals of modern society.

But they would think that, wouldn't they?

# 43 – The Breeding Ground

As someone with more than ten years of experience of fenced and more than ten years of experience of unfenced, I would be remiss if I didn't say that, in my experience, fenced relationships are a breeding ground for all kinds of problems and difficulties that just don't occur in unfenced relationships.

Here are a few comparisons between fenced and unfenced relationships (which as we've seen equate to the normal and natural planes).

## Jealousy & Possessiveness

• Fenced – Actively promotes jealousy and possessiveness.

• Unfenced – The twin-headed monster does not live here unless you invite him.

## Monopoly

• Fenced – If you want to have sex *at all* you have to establish a monopoly, which is essentially a sole-provider-of-sex agreement with one partner. There are several problems with that.

First, like all monopolies it blocks competition from other parties who could do the job better and with whom you might be happier. So regardless of how badly you or your partner perform your duties, or how much you take each other for granted, sex is (at least nominally) guaranteed. This is the root cause of stagnation by exclusivity.

Let's say your favourite food is pizza. How about if you were told you can eat pizza for breakfast, lunch and dinner every day for the rest of your life, but if you're ever, I mean EVER, caught eating anything other than pizza, then you're never allowed to eat pizza again!

We don't run our diets like that, so why would we run our sex lives like that?

What if you were pissed off with your partner and didn't want to deal with them but you really needed to have sex? Sex a basic human need after all.

That's like being in the mood for anything, and I mean ANYTHING, other than pizza. Imagine if you were really in the mood for BBQ ribs with french fries, and a good place for them was right on the way to the pizza place.

Well--you gotta trudge past the BBQ place as the tantalising scent of it teases your senses, with your head down muttering, "Pizza again." It won't be long before resentment builds and even the best pizza in the world, made in a proper wood-fired oven, begins to taste like stale cheese on toast.

These are moments of involuntary belonging. Moments of involuntary belonging are how resentment builds.

• Unfenced – You see each other and have sex with each other because you really want to, not because some kind of monopoly agreement is in place.

Every time you return to each other's arms, not only is it a choice, it's a *reaffirming* choice. There's no involuntary belonging, no resentment, no taking each other for granted, and no stagnation by exclusivity.

What if a lover doesn't return? Well, why would you want to be with someone who doesn't choose to be with you?

## Property

• Fenced – pussy is property; the Sex 2.0 deal was designed specifically to make it so. At least under Sex 3.0 it's a choice and not an obligation enforced by RD.

• Unfenced – pussy is not property.

## Cheating

• Fenced – Chances of relationships eventually becoming false-fenced are extremely likely--greater than 90% likelihood over a 30-year period.

• Unfenced – False-fenced is very unlikely. It would be possible only if both parties agreed to be unfenced but failed to kill the twin-headed monster and continued to do the jealousy and possessiveness thing.

## Infidelity

• Fenced – You can be sexually betrayed and cheated on, or be caught cheating. This usually means the end of the relationship and the loss of a valuable and genuine connection.

• Unfenced – There is no sexual betrayal in unfenced relationships. The worst that can happen is a partner can allow their sexuality to be roped into a fenced relationship with a third party, and you can find yourself frozen out.

In this case, as long as you don't react badly or in a jealous and possessive way, then the relationship ends up on "pause." It's often un-paused at a later date when the romantic infatuation phase with the third party runs its course or they break up.

## Love

• Fenced – In fenced relationships, love is conditional.

It's conditional on there being a fence, and on you not hopping over it while your partner isn't looking. Fenced relationships can be deceitful by their very nature.

The one kind of relationship that's more potentially deceitful than a conventional boyfriend/girlfriend relationship is a husband/wife relationship, because the punishment for getting caught is much higher. That can include loss of custody of children, of the family home and of half or more of net worth.

• Unfenced – In unfenced relationships, love is unconditional.

Call me crazy, but it seems that loving someone unconditionally is better. The only conditions that really apply in unfenced relationships are the same four principles that govern all healthy close relationships– communication, honesty, trust and respect.

## Fear

• Fenced – Fear of loss, of abandonment or of being replaced is greatly heightened because of the established exclusive sex-provider (monopoly) agreement.

This means that if you or—god forbid--your partner subsequently make the same agreement with somebody else, then you are out the door. Although you may feel wronged, it's also your own doing and you truly have nobody else to blame.

You agreed to a monopolistic, exclusive venture at the outset, and when nature dictates otherwise, you or your partner finds somebody else desirable enough to break the monopoly. Then the two of you have no choice other than to break up and go your separate ways.

To use the food analogy again, it's kind of like opening a restaurant, dedicating your life to creating the best, most charming and enticing restaurant you can, and then providing only one table and only one seat at the table.

• Unfenced – If you or your partner establish an unfenced relationship with someone else, it's fine.

The relationship is not based on exclusivity or ownership of sexual property, so as long as you continue to be attractive to each other and don't take each other for granted, there's no reason to fear loss, abandonment or being replaced.

There's no dynamic of "Who will it be, me or them?"

As mentioned earlier, there's a chance of being temporarily shut out, but in a landscape where you always have the option of hooking up with other partners and don't require permission to do so, there's no need to operate from the scarcity mentality that usually characterises a fenced relationship.

## Replacement

• Fenced – There's a danger of engaging in "binary" thinking in fenced relationships. That means that if you have a specific agenda--for example, if you want to have kids--you'll enter into all relationships with an either/or mentality (i.e. "either this person has to be the love of my life as well as the co-parent of my children, or I have to show them the door.")

This mode of thinking is necessary for getting what you want *only* because there's just one table at your restaurant and only one place to sit.

• Unfenced – No such danger in unfenced relationships.

## Scarcity

• Fenced – Once you've established a fenced relationship, the scarcity mentality that it promotes causes people to worry (sometimes obsessively) about the future nightmare scenario of being cheated on and having their heart broken.

If this has happened to them in a previous fenced relationship, that history increases the paranoia and makes people needier and overly dependent--both of which traits are massive turn-offs

This can often manifest itself as "policing behaviour" in relationships; checking your partner's phone/email etc.

Such behaviour, especially if done without the consent of your partner is dishonest, lacking in trust and is disrespectful.

• Unfenced – There's no policing behaviour in unfenced relationships. You can't patrol a fence that doesn't exist.

## Staying Friends

• Fenced – It's hard, if not impossible, to remain friends afterwards. Why?

When a fenced relationship breaks down, the frame that was set for how you relate to each other doesn't change, despite the breakup. Since your relationship was always based on the notion of sexual property, the twin-headed monster was in attendance at your every meeting, even though he may have been quietly in the background for much of the time.

When you try to remain friends after the breakup, the connection is a constant nagging reminder that your partner isn't your sexual property any more, and that your supposed guarantee of love and exclusivity went wrong. In other words, the twin-headed monster is ever present. Even if *you* don't feel this, there's a good chance that your ex does. With this kind of misery lurking in the background, the mutual reward that drives friendships is difficult if not impossible.

• Unfenced – Since the relationship has never been based on sexual ownership, the twin-headed monster never got the memo and never attended any of your meetings.

For that reason, long term unfenced relationships, even when they do break up (which is rare), don't suffer from this problem. There's no jealousy/possessiveness lurking around, and remaining friends afterwards is pretty easy.

## Money

• Fenced – Money arguments. This is a big one for many (though by no means all) couples in fenced relationships.

• Unfenced – No reason to mix your finances unless you intend to move in together or have a child. Even then, you're more likely to deal with that creatively because you're not operating from as many unexamined assumptions.

## Independence & Intimacy

• Fenced – Independence and intimacy are mutually exclusive.

With fenced relationships, people are taught they have to sacrifice one to get the other. They believe they must give up their freedom in order to have a long term relationship.

• Unfenced – Independence and intimacy are not mutually exclusive. Both are easily achievable at the same time in unfenced relationships.

## Nature

• Fenced – Fenced relationships offer only this choice: either pretend that people are monogamous by nature, or accept that they aren't but try to go against nature anyway.

• Unfenced – Unfenced relationships recognise that people are not monogamous by nature, and allow people to co-operate with nature.

## Honesty

• Fenced – Even if you're not the one to cheat, there's a good chance the relationship will end up false-fenced anyway. If you end up sharing your partner with somebody else, you won't know about it initially, and finding out about it may mean the end of the relationship.

• Unfenced – Since unfenced merely means no enforced monogamy (i.e. it's not synonymous with multiple partners), you may or may not have exclusivity. Either way it doesn't really matter too much, and there's no reason to be dishonest about it or to end the relationship over it.

## Blackmail

• Fenced – In fenced relationships, as your partner is your sole provider of sex it is possible, and not un-common, for people to withhold sex as a form of punishment when they don't get their own way; in other words, blackmail.

• Unfenced – Not possible. If sex is withheld, you just get it from elsewhere.

## Freedom

• Fenced – In fenced relationships, you need to break up with your partner to get your sexual freedom back--either that or go behind their back.

• Unfenced – With unfenced relationships you always have your sexual freedom. No deception is necessary and there's no reason to break up to get your sexual freedom back.

## Summary

When you take a look at the breeding ground, it's hard not to come to the conclusion that unfenced relationships are far more natural and honest than fenced relationships, and far less troublesome.

So how does that affect the dating game in the Sex 3.0 world?

# 44 – Dating in the Sex 3.0 Marketplace

In the Sex 3.0 marketplace, there are 3 dating modes:

    1 - Formal dating (fenced strategy)

    2 - Informal dating (mixed strategy)

    3 – Hanging out (unfenced strategy)

Let's take a look at all three:

## Formal Dating

A formal date is basically an audition. Essentially a guy is auditioning for the role of next boyfriend (in the fenced sense of the word).

In other words, he's trying out for the part of the next guy to take her sexuality, throw it in a box and label it as his property.

Formal dating sucks. It's a nightmare.

There are too many reasons to list for why, but to begin with its way too formal for really finding out about each other. Dinner and a movie? That means sitting across the table from each other with no physical contact, followed by watching a movie together where you can't even talk.

The knowledge that the guy is auditioning also makes women uncomfortable too because--and here's the crazy thing--even if she likes him she's going to be reluctant to sleep with him because she knows that, if things progress from there she'll be expected to give up her sexual freedom and get into the box. After all, both parties are very aware that they're out on a date. A woman is far more likely to have her guard up, and the vibe between them is more likely to be contrived and sexless.

This is one reason why formal dating has a very high failure rate.

## Informal Dating

No dinner, no movie, no formality, no pre-planned "pleasant evening together" to see if the guy can convince the girl to sacrifice her freedom.

Informal dating is a drink, a chat, it's relaxed, it's spontaneous, it's two people vibing and getting to know each other with no expectation that a formal arrangement may come out of it if they wind up in bed at the end of the night. A woman is far more likely to have her guard down, and the vibe between them is more likely to be flirty.

On an informal date, if a woman asks a guy if they're out on a *date*, a typical response might be "I don't know, let's not put a label on it. Let's just relax and see where things go."

Sex in a "no strings attached for now and let's see where things go from here" kind of way is the order of things, and that alone means it's far more likely to happen at the end of the night.

If the guy takes care of business between the sheets and the woman is left in a state of sexual bliss over the course of their initial encounters, all is good. If she likes the guy and she knows he likes her but is still left with at least some doubt about it, even better.

Women in this state are far more likely to want to get into the box. Informal dating has a high success rate. Women commonly try formal (sometimes online) dating for years and go on a string of formal dates only to find the guys "not suitable" and claim there's "no chemistry." Then they find themselves taken off the dating market by that one guy who they went on an informal date with.

The lesson here is that there's nothing worse for your dating prospects than actually labelling a date a *date*.

Informal dating is a mixed strategy which often leads to a short term unfenced sexual relationship with the expectation that, if they both like each other enough, then they will become fenced.

If they don't become fenced within the first few weeks or months then they will label the relationship as "going nowhere" or "not getting serious" and go their separate ways.

## Hanging Out

The first two modes relate to getting into fenced relationships in Sex 2.0, and they apply to fenced relationships in the Sex 3.0 marketplace as well. There's no real change here because the genetic imperatives do not change in the shift from Sex 2.0 to Sex 3.0 (although they did change from Sex1.0 to Sex 2.0.)

The category of hanging out specifically applies to unfenced relationships in the Sex 3.0 marketplace.

Since a date is an audition for the role of next boyfriend (in the conventional sense), and since that's not a role the unfenced are interested in auditioning for, the only option for those who are unfenced is to go out on a "hang out".

This mode is fundamentally different because, if you're a man, you have no desire whatsoever to fence in her sexuality, and you also don't plan stamp and label her as "my girlfriend." She can be *a* girlfriend, but never *my* girlfriend, because the word *my* is the possessive in English and you do not wish to possess her or to put her sexuality in a box, slam the lid shut and label it as your property.

If you're a woman in the unfenced mode, you have no desire to be labelled "my girlfriend" and no desire to enter into a relationship where enforced monogamy is the order of the day. The guy can be *a* boyfriend but never *my* boyfriend, and you ain't getting into any damn box.

This mode is fairly similar to informal dating and enjoys the same high level of success, but with the obvious wonderful additional benefit that at the end of it you're in an unfenced relationship.

On a hang out, if a woman asks a guy if they're out on a *date*, a typical response might be, "actually I don't date, but I do like to hang out with cool people, and whatever happens, happens."

Sex in a "no strings attached and let's see where things go from here" kind of way is the order of the things, and that means it's just as likely to happen at the end of the night as it is with informal dating.

As to where things go from here, this is where it gets interesting.

# 45 – Welcome to the Unfenced World

When two people have sex for the first time, unless they're very young or naïve, they don't automatically and immediately assume that they're officially a couple in the conventional sense of the word.

The feeling is more one of, "Oh, so we like each other in *that* way. Cool. Let's see where this goes."

In other words, at the beginning you have a grace period during which the frame of the relationship has not yet been set. This grace period is typically the first two to three weeks, or before you have seen and slept with each other more than a handful of times.

If you hook up with someone and you like them and want an unfenced relationship with them, then this grace period is the time to say so. This is very important, because once the frame of the relationship is set, it's *very* difficult to change afterwards.

Sometimes "the conversation" might come up spontaneously before you even sleep together which is fine too, but if it doesn't come up spontaneously then you need to introduce it during the grace period.

If you don't say anything deliberate during the grace period but keep seeing each other and sleeping together, certain assumptions are likely to be made and you'll probably by default end up in a conventional fenced relationship.

If an unfenced relationship is what you want, there are two key things to understand: how to introduce your beliefs, and how to present what you offer. Let's take a look at those.

## How to Introduce Your Beliefs

First, you'll be amazed at how open and receptive people are during this grace period to an alternative mindset with alternative possibilities--as long as you present these using the four pillars of pure-form relationships (communication, honesty, trust and respect).

It's crucial that:

### 1 - You truly and genuinely inhabit the mindset yourself

This part is impossible to fake (for long). Telling someone you believe in and practice unfenced relationships and then getting all jealous and possessive with them at the first sign of a "rival" makes you look like a big liar and a creep. Be congruent with what you say.

### 2 - You are totally honest from the beginning

Dishonesty, hiding things, and holding things back lead to lack of trust, which sets off the alarm bells more than does the alterative mindset itself. Just be honest and open. Honesty counts for a great deal, because when you're honest with people they know where they are emotionally and know they can trust you, even if they do find your lifestyle a bit strange.

Waiting till later to be honest, like well past the grace period and after certain assumptions have been made, doesn't work so well. Your lover may understandably feel deceived and angry, or feel like they've been misled.

### 3 - *You know how to present your mindset properly*

Relationships begin with communication. If unfenced relationships are what you're interested in, you have to present your mindset properly.

## How to Present Your Mind-set

One way to present your mind-set to a potential new partner is to give them this book. Obviously that's not required but it might not be a bad idea.

Unfortunately, since we've all grown up in a Sex 2.0 world, social training for setting out on happy, healthy, unfenced long term relationships (ULTRas) has been denied to us.

Ultimately your own social intelligence and conviction about your values will dictate whether you're successful or not, but check out these online resources at this book's address:

http://www.sexthreepointzero.com

At this website you'll find helpful articles and be able to chat online with others (including me) about the topics. How to present what you offer (and equally importantly, what you don't offer), comes down to three choices:

> 1 - You can make a **demand**
>
> 2 - You can make a **request**
>
> 3 - You can make a **statement**

An example of a demand is telling your lover you're unfenced, and if they don't like it that's tough; it's either your way or the highway.

This is not a very respectful way to speak to someone and I don't recommend it. Respect is one of the four pillars, and this goes against it.

The second option is to make a request. If you tell a new lover that you're into unfenced relationships, and explain what that means and ask if they would agree to you both being free to see other people, then you're making a **request** for what you want. This is kind of weak and I don't recommend it either. What do you say if they do mind?

The third option is to make a **statement,** and this I *do* recommend. Simply express that you offer only unfenced relationships, and state why.

There are plenty of reasons why you may prefer unfenced relationships, and enough of them have been covered in this book. You probably have other reasons of your own too. Great--state them.

For me personally, jealousy and possessiveness are two emotions that I don't enjoy. I don't want them in my life and relationships, and I don't enjoy following the five-step twin-headed monster sequence either. I usually I talk about that, but that's just me. The specific reasons *you* give don't matter, as long as what you're stating is really true for you.

To return to a food metaphor, you're simply stating what's on your menu and what isn't on your menu.

Make it clear that a fenced relationship with you is not available. If this is a source of disappointment, you can also state the good news that two other things missing from your menu are jealousy and possessiveness.

Simply stating what's on your menu works wonderfully well. People don't go into Pizza Hut and order a Big Mac and fries, because it's not on the menu. If they're told that they have to go to McDonalds for that, they don't shout and stamp their foot and insist that they want a Pizza Hut Big Mac and fries. That would be kind of crazy.

By stating what's on your menu, what you're offering is:

## Hobson's Choice

This is often misunderstood to mean no choice at all, but that's mistaken.

The saying originated with Thomas Hobson, an English stable owner. He rented out horses, and when customers entered the stable he offered them the choice of the horse in the stall nearest to the door, or no horse at all.[li]

Sometimes customers entered the stable and spotted another horse they desired and said "No, that one over there--the brown stallion with the white spots. I want that one." Hobson would smile, offer the horse in the nearest stall, and tell the customer to take it or leave it.

The reason Hobson offered this choice is not because he was a very stubborn man--it was because he was a very intelligent man.

The horses he hired out were sometimes gone for a long time and covered long distances, or a short time and covered short distances. He arranged the horses in the stables based on how much recovery time they needed, and rotated them so that the horse in the stall nearest the door was always the freshest and most well rested one.

Everybody wins with this system. The customer wins because they never have a horse that's too tired. The horses win because they never get so overworked and exhausted that they're good only for the glue factory. Hobson wins because his horses live longer.

Hobson's choice means offering the winning choice to all, and *never offering anything else*. This is the best way to approach unfenced relationships.

## Making the Transition to Unfenced

If you are not accustomed to unfenced relationships, but are interested in them, making the transition is really not that difficult.

Unfenced with a primary (most preferred) lover is a very popular choice. This was a strongly desired option with the women I interviewed, including ones already in a fenced relationship with a boyfriend.

If you're currently in a fenced relationship and want to make the transition to unfenced, well that cannot possibly succeed unless both parties are 100% on the same page. And you have to make it your first point of business to kill the twin-headed monster together.

That's not an easy task; starting a new relationship that's unfenced from the beginning is a piece of cake by comparison.

Unfenced becomes truly accepted only through living it, not by just reading or talking about it. You have to experience the reality to get a real sense of how it feels.

# 46 – Paint Your Life

The story of human sexual relationships across the ages is not that difficult to comprehend once you step back and look at the whole picture. We used to follow our nature, just like every species of animal that we share the planet with. Then we invented property and developed a set of social imperatives to deal with that.

The problem is that these social imperatives took us very far from the altar of nature, and in many cases operated in direct conflict with our genetic imperatives. To deal with that conflict we developed groupthink and relationship duress, and told ourselves that we are unique and special in this way, and so very intelligent. But that is a lie.

It's a lie against nature, and a narcissistic one at that. We are not so special as to be exempt from the laws of nature.

Nature did not blink and does not care about our lie. Nature doesn't change with popular opinion any more than truth changes when people believe it to be a lie.

Unnatural, unrealistic expectations for our sexual relationships are no more than an obstacle we placed in our own path, or a weight we strapped onto our own backs.

Society became very quick to tell us what it expected us to do, and very slow to explain the consequences of following its expectations.

This is a problem because you get only one life. You have only one canvas and one chance to paint it--with your paints, your brush strokes and your choices.

Submitting to society's expectations and the accompanying relationship duress is self-sabotage. It's like allowing someone to grab your wrist and make your brush strokes their brush strokes, painted in their way, even though it's not their canvas.

Of course the lie gradually began to unravel when, thanks to various social supports and effective contraception, people for the first time in ages actually had choice.

They had a choice to stop fighting nature without facing social expulsion, starvation or death as a result. They had a choice not to get in the way of nature.

Sexual relationships are exactly like all other kinds of relationships, in that they work until they don't.

The point at which relationships stop will now be dictated by the degree of mutual reward itself, rather than by any "until death do we part" promise. No amount of ceremonial self-rapture, even that sanctified by the church, has to trump our right to be ourselves.

Sex 3.0 means that we get to stop pretending and to start painting our own lives.

# 47 – Design and Morality

One of the main problems with the design of Sex 2.0 is that it lacks poetic dimension. I *love* great design and I love beauty.

Love has its own poetic beauty that speaks to the core of what is human in us all.

The design of Sex 2.0, on the other hand, is petty and full of ugliness: jealous possessiveness; sexual ownership; the struggle to assert paternity in a brutal manner that has caused countless cases of misery, mutilation, subjugation and death by murder or suicide. All this pain for the sake of....*stuff*? *Property?*

How absurd! It's even more absurd when you consider that it's no longer even necessary.

How ugly this design is! All of this ugliness drowns out the poetic beauty of truth, honesty, sexuality.

The whole thing is more than a little bizarre when you consider how obsessed people are with the design of their phone, toaster, car or laptop. Why then do we accept the ugly design of the far more important realm of sexual relationships?

## Sex 2.0 Morality

The morality of the Sex 2.0 world can be most clearly seen by looking at the heart of its design. As in pure-form relationships, Sex 2.0 rests on four pillars: fear, shame, guilt and deception.

## Fear

This is the big one. Sex 2.0 is fundamentally a fear-based design, for both men and women.

Men fear being cuckolded into raising someone else's child.

Women fear being labelled a slut and having "too much" sex—meaning an amount or variety that will damage their perceived value in the sexual marketplace.

## Shame

The conviction that what is sexual is shameful: what a great invention, huh? Sex is only, after all, one of the four basic needs for survival.

We are certainly unique as a species in that regard. Bravo! Well done us.

The systematic shaming of all those who fall outside the Sex 2.0 deal as sluts, whores, fags dykes, etc. is very Sex 2.0.

## Guilt

The idea of sex as sinful is also quintessentially Sex 2.0.

Guilt is different than shame in that it's an internal voice telling you that sex is wrong and bad or that *you* are wrong or bad just for being you. Not even necessarily for doing anything wrong but just for having "wicked" thoughts or even just desiring something–anything–that falls outside of the narrow and restrictive Sex 2.0 deal.

## Deception

Men cheat. They lie about it. Women cheat. They lie about it. Relationships that start as fenced and then become false-fenced are the norm in a Sex 2.0 society, but we lie to ourselves even further by pretending that hitched followed by a happily-ever-after fairy tale of lifetime monogamy is the norm.

Women routinely lie to themselves about their notch-count, or at least equivocate by coming up with all kinds of excuses as to why this or that encounter "didn't really count."

Both men and women are lied to by being told their entire lives that the most high-functioning sexual relationships, and the only legitimate kind, are the ones where you entrap yourselves in a walled garden where you're supposed to stay even when all the plants die. We are victims of this deception.

Deception and obligatory self-deception are at the heart of the Sex 2.0 design.

## Sex 3.0 Morality

Everything that is truly beautiful about sexual relationships lies without exception on the natural plane, not on the normal plane. The delightful flood of hormones when you kiss for the first time, the way a lover gazes longingly into your eyes, the touching, the flirtation, the foreplay, the penetration and the orgasm, the post-coital bliss as your lie in each other's arms freshly fucked and deeply satisfied.

Love--the heartfelt deep emotional need for the happiness and wellbeing of another human being--is truly human and truly natural.

The poetic dimensions of sexual relationships all lie on the natural plane, and the normal plane is the ugly artificial human construct that acts as a template imposed on top of it, against our will.

That construct acts as a lens we are forced to gaze though, which does nothing other than distort, drown out and corrupt so much of what we love in sexual relationships.

Beauty, truth, honesty and poetry in sexual relationships form the potent mix at the core of the Sex 3.0 design.

I don't mean love in a hippy-dippy way. Nor do I mean it in the corrupted Sex 2.0 kind of way that tells you that "love hurts," that you "always hurt the ones you love most," and that accepts that causing pain to another can be excused by saying you only did it because you love them so much.

When I say love I simply mean the deep emotional need for the wellbeing of another.

Fenced or unfenced? You choose. It's your damn life and don't let anyone tell you any different. It's none of their business.

## The Central Core

Sex 2.0 and Sex 3.0 are different right down to their central core.

The core of Sex 2.0 is control.

The core of Sex 3.0 is freedom of choice.

Sex 2.0's architecture is all designed around control. It's a fear-based system in which the need to control both causes and exacerbates human suffering.

Whenever someone's trying to control your sexuality, whether it's an individual or society at large, they're not acting in your interests. You cannot have true freedom of choice if you have relationship duress. You cannot have true freedom of choice if society deceives you or if you lie to yourself.

In the Sex 3.0 design, coercion and duress die and the things that define and guide your sexual relationships are the same things that guide and define all pure-form relationships.

## How Sex 3.0 Are You?

If you find that you have more affinity with the Sex 3.0 design than with the Sex 2.0 design, then maybe you're already more Sex 3.0 than you thought you were.

Are you the kind of person who uses relationship duress to tell others what they should or must do with their sexuality? Are you the kind of person who shames and stigmatises those who fall outside of the Sex 2.0 deal by calling them sluts, whores, fags, dykes or other names?

If not, that's good. It's pretty damn Sex 3.0 of you too. The Sex 2.0 deal is dead after all; no need for such nonsense.

Perhaps the greatest difference between the two is that in Sex 2.0 you're denying reality, and in Sex 3.0 you're acknowledging reality and playfully going along with it, which is far less painful and troublesome.

Sex 3.0 people face reality and make the most of it. They embrace nature instead of fighting it.

Acknowledge the fact that nature is constant and rock-solid-dependable. Recognise the truth of human nature. This will massively help you to live in tune with its benefits and to avoid the unpleasant consequences of violating it.

Ultimately Sex 3.0 is far superior than 2.0 because it makes it far easier to explore a path of non-harmfulness to oneself and to others and to alleviate the needless suffering of Sex 2.0.

# Free Bonus Materials

As a special thank you for buying and reading the book I am going to give you something *really* special.

I am going to give you access to something that, up until now, you could only get by booking one-on-one coaching sessions with me personally – the Sex 3.0 visual solution framework.

The book that you have just read deconstructs human sexuality, sexual psychology and sexual relationships as well as highlighting the many problems that we introduced into this realm with Sex 2.0.

All of the elements that you need to *reconstruct* human sexuality, sexual psychology and sexual relationships in a far superior form – Sex 3.0 – have been given to you by reading this book.

However, how about if I not only reconstruct it for you but I give you the entire visual solution framework for Sex 3.0 totally free?

This framework not only pulls *everything* together in a highly visual way but it is also an absolutely crucial tool that you can use to help you in the transition to Sex 3.0.

It can also be used by you to help others make the transition; friends, family, partners or students.

In other words it's been broken down and reconstructed into a visual framework that is *trainable*, that is *teachable*.

Not only I am going to give you this visual solution framework totally for free, I am going to walk you through the framework using online training videos and I am going to give you visual breakdowns of the differences between both Sex 2.0 and 3.0 but also the differences between fenced and unfenced relationships as well as a bunch of other cool free training material.

Sound good?

Point your web browser at the following address and follow the instructions from there:

**http://sexthreepointzero.com/framework/**

See you on the other side.

Love ... JJ

# About the Author

JJ Roberts is a former rock journalist from England who followed the standard script of conventional dating--what he terms "fenced" relationships--for the first half of his adult life. For the second half he has explored what he calls "unfenced" relationships, which are based on freedom rather than enforced monogamy.

The result was his first book, *Sex 3.0*, a fascinating insight into the modern-day fear-and-deception-based culture of Sex 2.0. Its replacement is Sex 3.0, which represents the death of fear and a return to nature.

*JJ Roberts*

# *Notes*

## Chapter 1 – This Book Is Not a Book

[i] http://en.wikipedia.org/wiki/Alfred_Korzybski

[ii] http://dictionary.reference.com/browse/duress?s=t

## Chapter 2 – Why Relationships Seem Difficult

[iii] http://www.youtube.com/watch?v=sno1TpCLj6A

## Chapter 4 – Relationships Defined In Just Two Words

[iv] http://dictionary.reference.com/browse/relationship?s=t

## Chapter 7 – Sex 1.0

[v] http://en.wikipedia.org/wiki/Hunter-gatherer

[vi] http://en.wikipedia.org/wiki/Hunter-gatherer#Common_characteristics

## Chapter 8 – Nature's Desire

[vii] http://www.bbc.co.uk/news/science-environment-14616161

[viii] http://en.wikipedia.org/wiki/Extinction

## Chapter 9 – Why Does Sex Exist?

[ix] http://en.wikipedia.org/wiki/Asexual_reproduction

[x] http://ferrebeekeeper.wordpress.com/2011/05/16/turkeys-and-parthenogenesis/

[xi] http://www.bbc.co.uk/news/science-environment-14046316

[xii] http://www.sciencemag.org/content/333/6039/216.abstract


Chapter 11 – The Sex 1.0 Marketplace
[xiii] http://en.wikipedia.org/wiki/Neolithic_Revolution


Chapter 13 – Marriage, the Sex 2.0 Deal
[xiv] Stephanie Coontz, "Marriage, a History" Penguin Books (February 28, 2006)

[xv] http://en.wikipedia.org/wiki/Writing_system#History_of_writing_systems

[xvi] http://en.wikipedia.org/wiki/Abrahamic_religions

[xvii] Stephanie Coontz, "Marriage, a History" Penguin Books (February 28, 2006)

[xviii] http://en.wikipedia.org/wiki/Shamanism

[xix] http://en.wikipedia.org/wiki/Paganism


Chapter 15 – The Sex 2.0 Genetic Imperative
[xx] http://en.wikipedia.org/wiki/Hypergamy


Chapter 16 – The Sex 2.0 Marketplace
[xxi] http://en.wikipedia.org/wiki/Human_bonding#Pair_bonding


Chapter 18 – Relationship Duress
[xxii] http://en.wikipedia.org/wiki/No-fault_divorce


Chapter 21 – Monogamy Is a Sexual Perversion

xxiii http://www.msnbc.msn.com/id/17951664/ns/health-sexual_health/t/many-cheat-thrill-more-stay-true-love/#.UGHchlF7SSp

Chapter 22 – The Pacman, the Slut and the Whore

xxiv http://en.wikipedia.org/wiki/List_of_sovereign_states_by_date_of_formation

xxv http://www.etymonline.com/index.php?term=harlot

xxvi http://www.etymonline.com/index.php?term=slut

Chapter 23 – How Did We Get Into This Mess?

xxvii http://en.wikipedia.org/wiki/Groupthink

Chapter 28 – Feminism Is Dead, and How Feminists Killed It

xxviii http://en.wikipedia.org/wiki/Suffrage

xxix http://www.etymonline.com/index.php?term=misogynist

xxx http://www.etymonline.com/index.php?term=misandry

xxxi http://www.etymonline.com/index.php?term=sexist

Chapter 29 – Men and Women Cheat For Different Reasons

xxxii http://en.wikipedia.org/wiki/Coolidge_effect

xxxiii http://www.heretical.com/wilson/coolidge.html

xxxiv http://www.springerlink.com/content/w842421446614n40/

xxxv http://moreintelligentlife.com/content/issues-ideas/catherine-nixey/whos-daddy

xxxvi http://www.msnbc.msn.com/id/17951664/ns/health-sexual_health/t/many-cheat-thrill-more-stay-true-love/#.UGHchlF7SSp

Chapter 30 – The Breakdown of the Sex 2.0 Deal

xxxvii http://moreintelligentlife.com/content/issues-ideas/catherine-nixey/whos-daddy

xxxviii http://en.wikipedia.org/wiki/DNA#History_of_DNA_research

Chapter 32 – Groupthink and the Breakdown of The Sex 2.0 Deal

xxxix http://en.wikipedia.org/wiki/Groupthink#Symptoms

Chapter 36 – Slaying the Twin-Headed Monster

xl http://www.msnbc.msn.com/id/17951664/ns/health-sexual_health/t/many-cheat-thrill-more-stay-true-love/#.UGHchIF7SSp

Chapter 37 – The Death of the Pacman, the Slut and the Whore

xli http://www.dna-geneticconnections.com/dna_accuracy.html

Chapter 38 – The Death of Relationship Duress

xlii http://en.wikipedia.org/wiki/Madonna%E2%80%93whore_complex

xliii http://en.wikipedia.org/wiki/Dogma

Chapter 40 – Belonging in a Sex 3.0 World

xliv http://en.wikipedia.org/wiki/Slavery

xlv http://en.wikipedia.org/wiki/Slavery#Abolitionism

xlvi http://en.wikipedia.org/wiki/Hypergamy

xlvii Stephanie Coontz, "Marriage, a History" Penguin Books (February 28, 2006)

Chapter 42 – Marriage in the Sex 3.0 Marketplace

xlviii http://en.wikipedia.org/wiki/Civil_solidarity_pact

xlix http://en.wikipedia.org/wiki/Civil_solidarity_pact#Figures

l http://www.emirates247.com/news/region/saudi-arabia-has-a-divorce-every-30-minutes-2011-04-10-1.379100

Chapter 45 – Welcome to the Unfenced World

[li] http://en.wikipedia.org/wiki/Hobson%27s_choice

Made in the USA
San Bernardino, CA
08 April 2013